The Trial of Anne Hutchinson

"Reacting to the Past" Series

The Trial of Anne Hutchinson

Liberty, Law, and Intolerance in Puritan New England

Second Edition

Michael P. Winship
University of Georgia

Mark C. Carnes
Barnard College
Columbia University

W. W. Norton & Company
New York   London

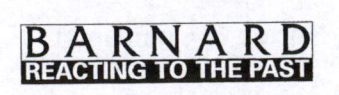

W. W. Norton & Company has been independent since its founding in 1923, when William Warder Norton and Mary D. Herter Norton first published lectures delivered at the People's Institute, the adult education division of New York City's Cooper Union. The firm soon expanded its program beyond the Institute, publishing books by celebrated academics from America and abroad. By mid-century, the two major pillars of Norton's publishing program—trade books and college texts—were firmly established. In the 1950s, the Norton family transferred control of the company to its employees, and today—with a staff of four hundred and a comparable number of trade, college, and professional titles published each year—W. W. Norton & Company stands as the largest and oldest publishing house owned wholly by its employees.

Production Manager: Ashley Horna

Library of Congress Cataloging-in-Publication Data

Carnes, Mark C. (Mark Christopher), 1950– author.
   The trial of Anne Hutchinson : liberty, law, and intolerance in Puritan New England / Michael P. Winship, Mark C. Carnes.—[Revised Edition].
      pages cm.—(Reacting to the Past / Barnard)
   Includes bibliographical references.
   ISBN 978-0-393-93733-6 (paperback)
   1. Hutchinson, Anne, 1591–1643—Trials, litigation, etc.   2. Freedom of Religion—Massachusetts—History—17th century.   3. Massachusetts—History—Colonial period, ca. 1600–1775.   4. Puritans.   I. Winship, Michael P. (Michael Paul), author.   I. Title.
   KF223.H86C37 2014
   345.73'0288—dc23

                                                                                   2013042603

W. W. Norton & Company, Inc., 500 Fifth Avenue, New York, NY 10110
wwnorton.com

W. W. Norton & Company Ltd., Carlisle Street, London W1D 3BS

3 4 5 6 7 8 9

CONTENTS

Sin and Salvation

> Of every tree of the garden thou mayest freely eat, but of the tree of the knowledge of good and evil, thou shalt not eat of it . . .

The pastor glances at the Bible. His arms are anchored to the lectern. He seems unaware of the multitude seated on benches before him. Several are taking notes, quills scratching. Perhaps in the musty gloom he cannot make out the faces of the living saints assembled in the church. The other people of Boston—those who do not belong to his church and yet are obliged to attend—sit in the deep shadows in the back, far behind you. The morning sun has doubtless burned off the fog from the harbor, but few of its rays have seeped around the tight shutters of the church's windows.

> Now the serpent was more subtle than any beast of the field . . .

He raises his eyebrows, observes the assemblage, and blinks, as if in surprise at seeing so many people. Then he looks to the ceiling, reciting from memory:

> . . . the woman said unto the serpent, "We may eat of the fruit of the trees of the garden, but of the fruit of the tree which is in the midst of the garden, God hath said, 'Ye shall not eat of it, neither shall ye touch it, lest ye die.'"

He draws this last word into several syllables—an affectation, perhaps, that they taught at Cambridge—and then his voice trails off. You wonder: Were Adam and Eve originally happy? Or even before the serpent, were they, too, plagued with sleepless nights?

> And the serpent said unto the woman, "Ye shall not surely die: For God doth know that in the day ye eat of this fruit, then your eyes shall be opened, and ye shall be as gods, knowing good and evil". And when the woman saw that the fruit of the tree was good . . .

A man in the back has been coughing, and now he hacks violently. The pastor pauses, and the sudden silence is unnerving. Last winter, a coughing illness had carried away nearly a dozen people. The ground had been frozen too hard to bury the dead properly, except for the infants, whose graves could be hewn from the turf with a hatchet. No winter in England was ever like this.

> . . . she took of the fruit thereof, and did eat, and gave also unto her husband with her; and he did eat. And the eyes of them both were opened, and they knew that they were naked; and they sewed fig leaves together, and made themselves aprons.

That word—apron! You jolt to attention.

> And they heard the voice of the Lord God walking in the garden in the cool of the day . . .

You still feel the flaxen cloth, stiff and scratchy, against your cheek. Before the service, while you were repairing a loose floor plank near the pulpit, she came toward you with an hourglass and raised it to place on the pulpit. She could not quite reach. Stretching on her toes, she leaned slightly forward. Her hip pressed against your cheek. You felt its curve beneath the coarse cloth. Her apron brushed your lips, and for an instant she swayed against you for balance. You felt her muscles tighten as she reached still higher. You could scarcely breathe, and you fixed your eyes on the floorboard. Then she briskly walked away. You swallowed.

> And God said, "Hast thou eaten of the tree, whereof I commanded thee that thou shouldest not eat?"

You stare at the pastor, wide-eyed, stricken with guilt. You expect him to hold out a bony hand and point it at you. But he ignores you, absorbed in the text of Genesis.

> . . . And the woman said, "The serpent beguiled me, and I did eat."

Now the truth comes to you. He who speaks to you is not the pastor, but God!

> Unto the woman, He said, "I will greatly multiply thy sorrow and thy conception; in sorrow thou shalt bring forth children, and thy desire shall be to thy husband, and he shall rule over thee." And unto Adam He said, "Because thou hast hearkened unto the voice of thy wife, and hast eaten of the tree, of which I commanded thee . . ."

Another flurry of coughs, and you glance toward the shadows in the back. Some of those people, too, may be dead and buried before the spring rains have softened the earth.

> . . . "Cursed is the ground for thy sake; in sorrow shalt thou eat of it all the days of thy life. Thorns also and thistles shall it bring forth to thee; and thou shalt eat the herb of the field. In the sweat of thy face shalt thou eat bread, till thou return unto the ground; for out of it wast thou taken: for dust thou art, and unto dust shalt thou return."

The sin of Adam and Eve—the Original Sin—had doomed all mankind forever. In the shadows, you see that a child is spitting into a wad of leaves. Then, in turning back toward the pastor, you catch a glimpse of her. You had resolved not to look. You reproach yourself for doing so now. But you look. Her head is bowed, her hair bound and covered with a bonnet. A few wayward strands curl around the nape of her neck and touch her ear.

You again force yourself to breathe.

The pastor has paused. Now he looks up and raises his arms, as if to embrace the people of Boston. You can't figure out which words are his and which are those of the Bible.

> We must see sin clearly. We must see it clearly in its own nature, its native color and proper hue. We are all sinners.

He glances at the Bible, as if for confirmation. Then he brings his hands toward his body and taps his fingers against his chest repeatedly.

It is my infirmity. I cannot help it. My weakness, I cannot be rid of it. No man lives without faults and follies; the best have their failings. But it's one thing to say sin is thus and thus, another thing to see it to be such. . . It is one thing to see a disease in the book or in a man's body . . .

Now his hands, fingers crimped, clutch at the air—

. . . Another to **find** and **feel** it in a man's self.

Now they dig into his shirt.

There is the report of it.

He airily gestures toward the shadows in the back—

. . . and **here**.

–his hands close into fists and beat against his heart—

. . . and **here,** the malignity and venom of it.

You look at your hands and see that your fists are also clenched. You force your fingers to relax. You look around. No one has noticed. Again your eyes are drawn to her. You do not look away. You cannot look away. A fluttering shaft of light from the lamp silhouettes her face; her hair has a soft chestnut sheen.

. . . Sin is the greatest evil in the world, or indeed that can be. For that which separates the soul from God, that which brings all evils of punishment and makes all evils truly evil, and spoils all good things to us, that must needs be the greatest evil. This is the nature of sin . . .

As a child you had often heard the story of "the fall" of Adam and Eve. You had thought of their "fall" as a literal event, like Jack and Jill tumbling down the hill. And you always associated it with an afternoon long ago when you were a child in England. Your family had gone for a walk along a bluff overlooking the ocean. You strayed toward the edge and leaned out, hand against a large rock. Then you looked down.

In that instant, you were seized by raw terror. Far below, the heaving swells of the ocean slammed into boulders, shattering into white spumes; a deep, continuous rumble shook the face of the cliff. At the center of this violence was a smooth black pool. Though frozen with fear, you craned your neck to see better. Despite your terror—or perhaps because of it—the pool beckoned. At that instant, the story of Adam and Eve made sense. They had fallen into a place such as that, a long, hurtling plunge to utter destruction.

When thou considerest but thy course, dost thou not wonder that the great and terrible God doth not pash such a poor insolent worm to powder and send thee packing to the pit every moment?

In that childish vision, you saw your destiny: The black pool was the pit of your doom. Yet you sneak another glance. Her eyes are closed tight, perhaps in prayer, her hands folded upon her lap.

Over the years, you have come to see that pool with unforgettable clarity. Its darkness is deeper than black, a glassy sheen like a night sky before a storm. Death, you realize, will not be a falling into the grave and a gradual yielding of the body to the dust from which it came. Rather, death is a swallowing up in the black abyss of God's wrath, terror mounting—infinitely mounting—with the soul forever denied the shattering release of physical destruction.

The evening after the family outing—after you had stared into the abyss—the family gathered around the table to read the Bible. When your turn came, your mother handed it to you. And without looking, you opened to Jeremiah 46 and read: "But fear not thou, O my servant Jacob, and be not dismayed, O Israel: for, behold, I am with thee." Then you understood. God was with you. You were among the elect, those saved from the abyss.

> They whose hearts are pierced by the ministry of the word, they are carried with love . . .

The minister's words again resonate with your thoughts! All these years, you have been carried with God's love. Christ had died on the cross to give you eternal life. You imagined that such love must know no bounds, but God's love DID have limits. A few months ago, while visiting the Boston Church, the famous John Cotton had preached that the saints of God were few in number: probably only ten from any church would likely be among the elect; the rest would end up in the black abyss of eternal torment. That day, you glanced around and counted: Cotton, indisputably; surely Governor John Winthrop, who was behind this whole venture to New England. But then you stopped. You did not know how others felt and thought, but you knew then that you were among the elect.

You are about to look again in her direction, but you stop yourself. And you draw comfort from that. Your restraint—doesn't that prove that God has elected you for salvation? Some of the ministers have made exactly this point. Only those who have received God's grace can truly ward off temptation. Because of that grace—and the love of God from which it flows—such persons find it easier to follow in His footsteps. They behave in a godly fashion because they have been chosen by God as His saints. Their holiness—or sanctification, as the minister calls it—is evidence of their redemption by God, or their justification, to use the Biblical term. But you recall that Mrs. Hutchinson—that keen small woman with the clever tongue—had denounced exactly this idea when you and some others went to her house. She said that such a belief was a big step on the path to the corruption of Catholicism. People who think that saintly behavior is proof of God's grace will soon imagine that, if they behave according to God's word and laws, they can persuade God to grant them salvation. Soon they will be invoking the assistance of priests to plead with God, or they will try to bribe God by building great temples with stained glass windows and gaudy altars to honor His name. What foolish presumption, she had said. These "legal Christians"—she spat out the words—do not deceive God. They probably don't even deceive themselves. They know, she added, nodding her head, that God has not graced their lives.

Again, you have an urge to look behind you. But if God has graced your life and made you one of His saints, would you still have such base urges? Perhaps when God revealed the abyss when you were a child, He was foreshadowing the destruction that was to be your destiny. And, as you fight the urge to look at her, you know that you are wicked. And then there are the dreams: over and over again, falling, tumbling down into the pit, a terror that knows no bottom. Is this not proof of your damnation?

But your minister, and most of the others from the colony who preached at your church, said that God's elect commonly experienced such doubts. He himself has talked about his own struggles and doubts. He advised you to study the Bible, to seek guidance from him and other ordained ministers, to become a vital part of God's church, and to scrutinize your actions and thoughts. After a bout of anxiety, those who were truly of the elect would be likely to again find comfort and assurance. And, just as likely, they would again doubt; they might even find themselves in despair, convinced that they were going to hell. This process could be grueling and protracted. For many, it never ended. But it was normal. From sin and doubt would come renewed strength—God's gift to the elect. Reinvigorated by this God-given strength, you would scrutinize your actions and thoughts. You would thank God for giving you the strength to doubt and to better yourself. You breathe a bit more easily in thinking of this.

But then you recall the words of Mrs. Hutchinson. She had said that God's grace was not about struggle but about love. When He saved you, He embraced you with His love. You knew that He had done so. You might miss the first sign or perhaps the next one, but God's grace was overwhelming. Those who tasted God's love directly could never forget it, and the remembrance of it changed them forever. Mrs. Hutchinson said that those who were plagued with doubts surely doubted for good reason: They were likely damned.

Are you among the damned? The orthodox ministers—those opposed to Mrs. Hutchinson—say that it is Anne Hutchinson and her listeners who deceive themselves. Only those who have received God's grace can truly search their souls for the wickedness that is in all mortals. Only those who have been justified will torment themselves over their failings and inadequacies. Only those who are among God's saints will demand of themselves that they behave—in mind and deed—in ways that accord with God's will. A momentary lapse and—without thinking—you turn your head. Hers remains bowed, her eyes still shut. She is pale, more so than before. More strands have escaped from her bonnet, and you notice a soft down on her neck. You want to push the curls back into the bonnet and perhaps trail your finger along her neck.

We have looked over the loathsome abominations that lie in his bosom . . .

The minister's voice thunders.

Does it make sense that God's saints should be wracked with guilt and anxiety? Mrs. Hutchinson spoke of a joy unlike any that could be found among earthly pleasures. Such was the gift He gave to His elect. The holy John Cotton said something similar from this very same pulpit. You cannot be truly godly until you have been touched by God's free gift of grace. Your good thoughts and deeds are mere playacting, an attempt to persuade yourself and others that you are good. Perhaps you playact in an effort to persuade God—what ludicrous folly! Can there be any more damning proof of one's sin? You sense a movement and look toward her. Her husband leans back and blocks your view, but he moves forward and you see her again. She has raised her head. Her eyes open and she looks at you. For an instant, your eyes lock. Then she looks down.

You feel your throat tighten. The awful doubts about yourself and your fate return. Has God ever loved you or have you been fooling yourself? Will you ever find true assurance of His love? Or when you die, will you slip into the abyss, ever falling?

Note: The quotes are from the first few paragraphs of the King James Bible, the Book of Genesis. The pastor's words are from a sermon by Thomas Hooker, "A True Sight of Sin." Hooker preached briefly in Cambridge and moved to Connecticut in 1635. The narrator is fictional.

Introduction: The Trial of Anne Hutchinson

The place is Cambridge, in the Massachusetts Bay Colony. The year is 1637, in early November. The exceptionally harsh winter has already set its icy grip on the colony, but this has done little to cool the passions of many of the 8,000 English settlers. Yesterday the General Court of Massachusetts Bay, Governor John Winthrop presiding, convicted Mrs. Anne Hutchinson of slandering the colony's ministers. The official record of her trial stated that "shee declared voluntarily her revelations for her ground, & that shee should bee delivered & the Court ruined, with their posterity, & thereupon was banished." [A record of the trial is included with this packet.] Two male allies had been previously banished. Because winter has set in, her banishment has been delayed until spring. Hutchinson's friends, cemented to her by the force of her convictions and power of her mind, cherish her as a voice of religious fervor in a community that has lost sight (or so they believe) of the ideals that drove them across the Atlantic. Some have threatened to leave Massachusetts Bay Colony; others remain restive. At stake is not just one woman's fate, but the nature of each puritan's relationship to God and to each other.

Maps

MAP 1: PURITAN BOSTON, 1637

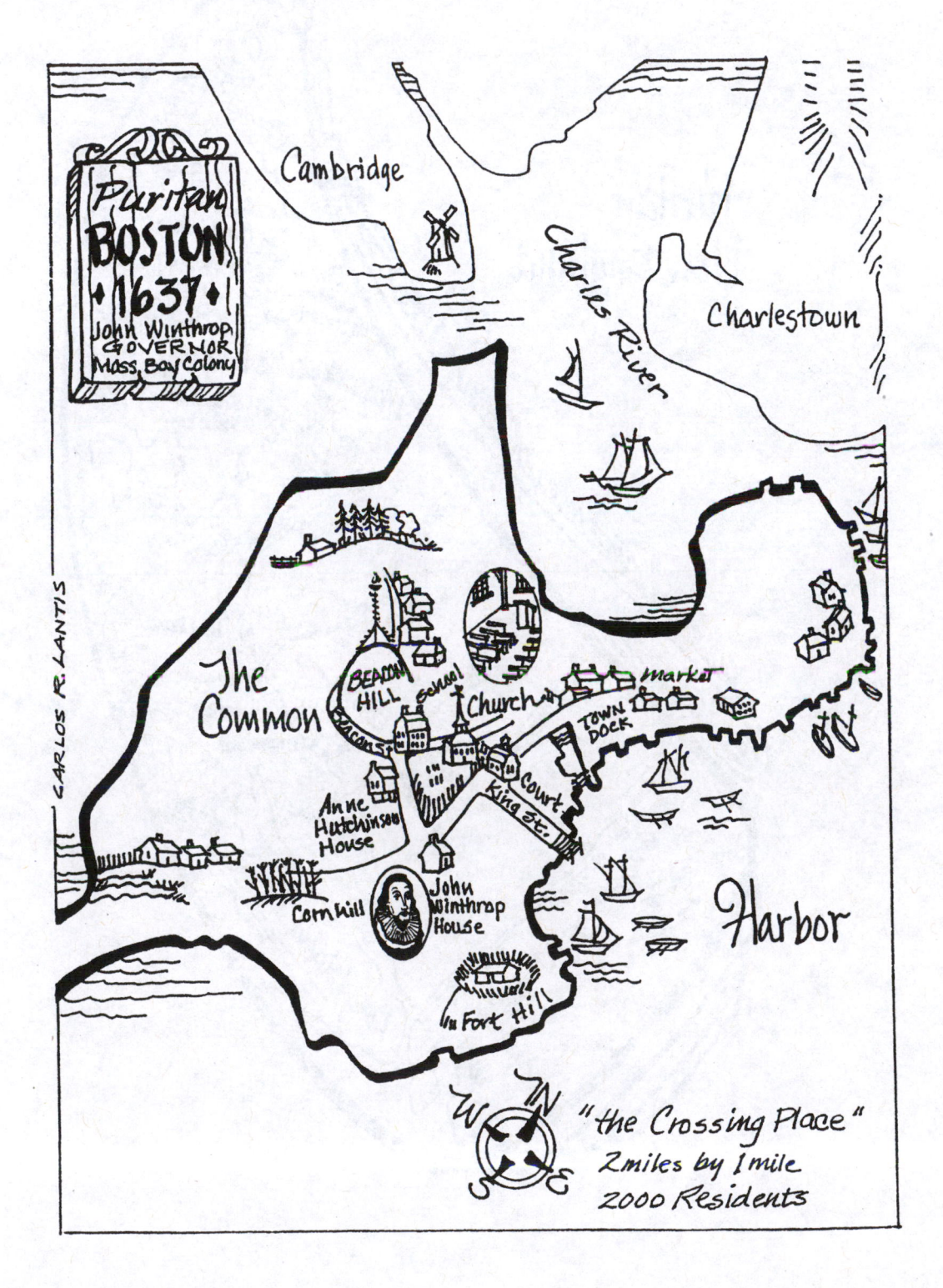

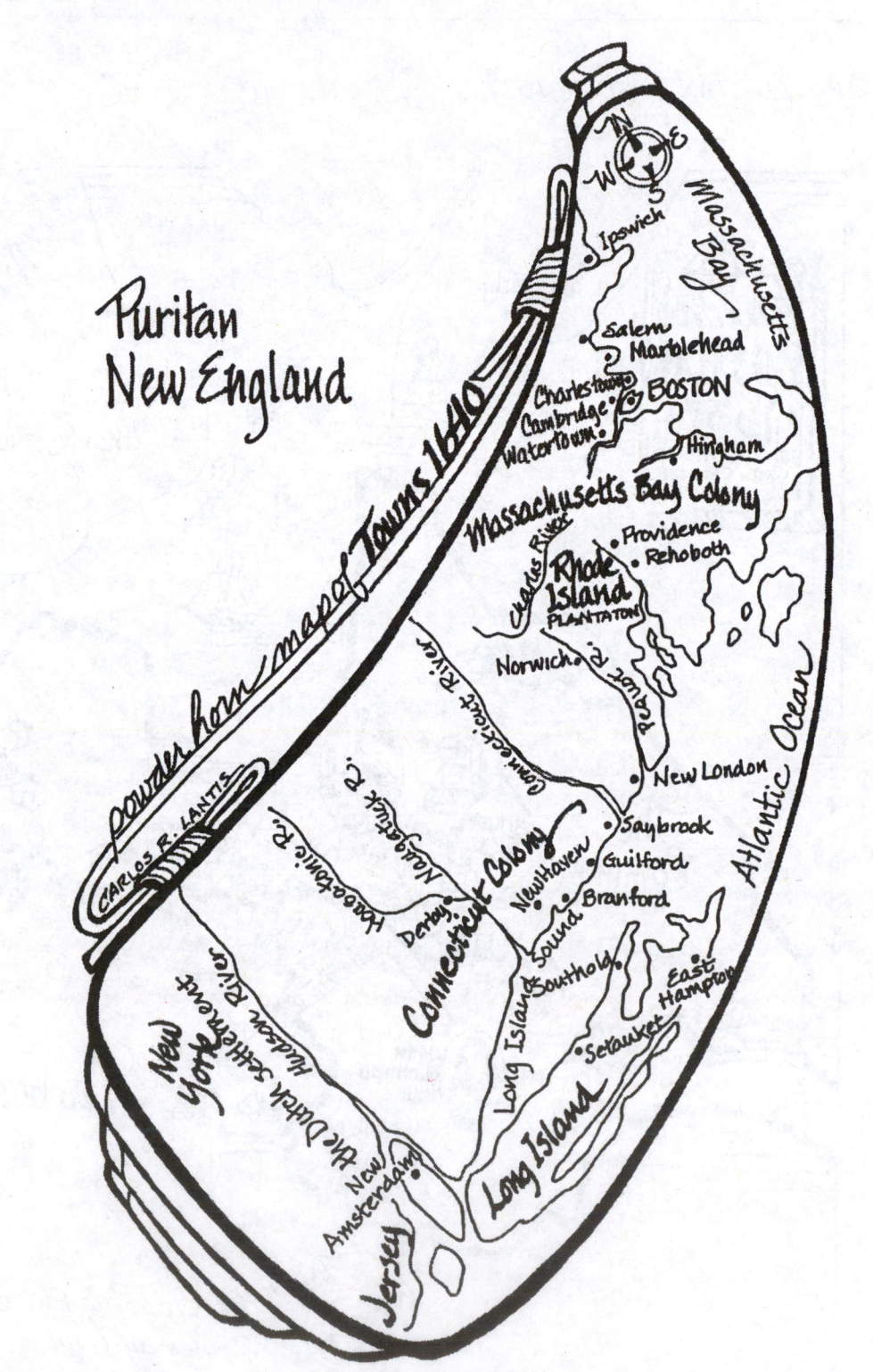

Puritan
New England

The Game Itself

THE GAME PREMISE: A COUNTERFACTUAL HYPOTHESIS

The game that will be played during the next few weeks is based on these materials surrounding the trial of Anne Hutchinson. However, the game is based on three counterfactual premises: The first is that, due to the protests of her supporters during her trial, the Court decided that very same day to take the precaution of disarming any male who had shown significant sympathy for her or Wheelwright (the disarming took place in fact two weeks later). The second is that on the morning after Hutchinson's trial, Massachusetts' most prominent and honored minister, John Cotton, appears before the General Court. Until recently, he has been a strong supporter of Hutchinson. At her trial yesterday, he was conflicted, defending her at times and lapsing into silence at other crucial moments (as the record shows). He is still not sure if she deserved her conviction. This morning, he is requesting that the General Court review its decision for his own reasons, not in the least of which is it will help him make up his mind. Winthrop and the other leaders value Cotton immensely, and they certainly do not want to do anything that might provoke him to leave Massachusetts, as he almost did a few months previously.

The General Court agrees that it will commence its review of its decision immediately. Thus the game will not be a recapitulation of the actual trial of Mrs. Hutchinson. It will be a debate over the reasons for, and justice of, her conviction and sentence and a decision on whether that conviction and sentence should stand or be replaced. The stability—and perhaps the survival—of the colony depends on that decision being widely perceived among the colonists as just and fair. (The reason for this counterfactual premise is to allow students to cite the evidence and record presented at the **first** trial. In point of historical fact, Mrs. Hutchinson was tried a second time in March 1638, though this time the trial was held within the Boston Church, and the issue was whether to excommunicate her before banishment. This second church trial, and the events and disclosures preceding it, are presumed **not** to have occurred for the purposes of the game. Students may not cite evidence submitted in that 1638 trial, which is set in November 1637.)

A third premise is that a shipload of immigrants has arrived in Massachusetts Bay Colony while the General Court was meeting, and they have the potential of changing the balance. This is not inconsistent with the historical record. The General Court was worried enough about the opinion of immigrants that it even passed a law allowing magistrates to interrogate and exclude immigrants who were found deficient. These issues, too, will figure prominently in the game.

MAJOR GROUPS IN THE GAME

The game will have three major types of roles:

> The Friends of (Mrs.) Anne Hutchinson, who will seek to prove not just that the trial was unfair, but that Anne's religious views could not be seditious because they accorded with the will of God;

Governor John Winthrop, the Pastor of the Boston Church, and their supporters, who will seek to preserve their godly commonwealth by making a stern example of wild-eyed religious zealots such as Hutchinson; and

A group of English immigrants to Massachusetts who missed the trial because they arrived as it was taking place. They yet may influence the outcome of the General Court.

ABOUT THE TRIAL

This is not a trial in the sense of an objective legal proceeding: No courtroom tricks are likely to prevail. The General Court was primarily not a law court, but a legislative assembly comprised of elected representatives of all Massachusetts Bay. Since Massachusetts Bay Colony was explicitly conceived as a puritan enterprise, religious values could override legal ones. To put it somewhat differently: Views that were religious anathema to puritans necessarily posed a danger to the puritan state; views that were religiously sound took precedent over the immediate concerns of the state.

In addition to the proceedings held by the General Court, some of the class sessions will be meetings of the congregation of the **Boston Church**. These meetings, which will be called as necessary, will determine which **immigrants** will be admitted as members of the church. Membership has political significance, too, because only members of a local congregation acquire political rights (such as voting and office holding) and can become members of the General Court. All immigrants who are admitted to the church automatically are presumed to have been elected to the General Court as well.

The classes themselves will consist of meetings of either the General Court or the Boston congregation. Probably both will be held at the same session, but the same person will not preside. Massachusetts Bay Colony was not a theocracy: That is, the clergy did not rule the colony. But it was a puritan commonwealth, which meant that the civil agency—the government—worked hand in glove with the orthodox puritan ministry and vice versa. (Orthodox here means those who opposed Wheelwright and Hutchinson.) Thus clergy are free to speak and vote on the General Court (in fact, they could not be members of the General Court and spoke only when invited to do so). Winthrop, as in real life, can speak to the Boston congregation and vote in church matters.

The evidence in the November proceeding consisted chiefly of depositions by Anne Hutchinson and by the ministers of the colony. (A record of this testimony is included in the game packet.) The points at issue all pertained to the proper interpretation of puritan dogma. To attain your objective, you must become proficient in the religious ideas and worldview of seventeenth-century New England. But you should remember, as did Winthrop—incessantly—that the puritan theological debate occurs in a community that is coping with profound economic change as well as extreme natural phenomena: brutal winters, unfamiliar crops and diseases, and other dangers. There is always a chance that, if religious disputes become too divisive, the community's economy will collapse, or the colony will fall prey to famine, disease, or even the Indians. Or King Charles may send a fleet to install a new governor who will adhere to his principles, most of which are opposed to the puritans'.

Schedule of Classes

SUMMARY TABLE: DATE AND SEQUENCE OF CLASSES				
Class Date	Class #	Student tasks BEFORE Class	Class Activities	Activities of General Court or Boston Church
	1 (Preparatory Session A)	All of student packet except for primary documents	Introduction: historical context of Massachusetts Bay Colony; election of Governor Winthrop	None: Setup
	2 (Preparatory Session B)	Read primary documents and reread theology section	Discussion of puritan theology; distribution of remaining roles and faction meetings for Winthropians and Hutchinsonians; assignment of "indeterminate" roles; additional role sheets given to Deputy Governor General, Pastor, Assistant Pastor, and First Friend of Anne	None: Setup
	3 (Preparatory Session C)	Begin preparation of paper 1	Faction meetings; instructor meets individually with indeterminates; First Friend of Anne and Pastor/Winthrop meet to discuss paper presentation sequence	
	4 (Game Session 1)	Work on paper 1	Reminder: students to post papers on Web site	*Church*: Sermon by Pastor; 2 immigrants present petitions; *Court*: Statement by Winthrop; several Hutchinsonians present initial arguments
	5 (Game Session 2)	Read submissions from previous class	Reminder: students to post papers on Web site	*Church*: presentation of 2 more immigrant petitions; Hutchinsonians may respond to Pastor's sermon; *Court*: Winthropian and Hutchinsonian presentations
	6 (Game Session 3)	Read previous submissions; begin paper 2	All students, except Cotton, have submitted a first paper or petition by end of this session	*Church*: More immigrant petitions; *Court*: more debate

	7 (Game Session 4)	Paper 2 due	Reminder: students to post second papers on Web site	*Church*: More immigrant re-petitions; *Court*: more debate
	8 (Game Session 5)	Read submissions from previous class	Reminder: students to post second papers on Web site	*Court*: more debate
	9 (Game Session 6)	Read submissions from previous class	Ensure that all students (except Cotton) have submitted a second paper by end of this session.	*Court*: final presentations; last presentation: Sermon by John Cotton; vote on guilt or innocence of Anne Hutchinson; game ends
	10 (Post-mortem)	None	Discussion of what transpired; Cotton's sermon due	

CLASS 1 (PREPARATORY SESSION A): INTRODUCTION AND ELECTION OF WINTHROP

Come to class having read game packet (except the appendices).

Toward the end of this class, the instructor will stop the discussion and open class for nomination and election of Governor Winthrop. The instructor will first indicate which students, by virtue of their leadership roles in previous games or their special time commitments in the weeks to come, are excluded from nomination. After at least two nominations have been received, all students will vote by secret ballot to elect Governor Winthrop. If there are more than two nominations, the process will be repeated, with lowest vote total eliminated, until one student receives an absolute majority. She will then be given the Winthrop role packet. The student elected as Winthrop should not discuss her role with any other student until after the remaining roles have been assigned (next class).

CLASS 2 (PREPARATORY SESSION B): DISCUSSION OF PURITANISM; DISTRIBUTION OF ROLES

Reread game packet, especially the theology section, and also read all of the documents.

After the discussion of puritanism, and when about 25 minutes remain in class, the instructor will distribute the remaining role sheets to students (in envelopes, preferably), though students are not to open or read their roles until the Gamemaster is satisfied with the allocation of roles. After the Gamemaster directs students to read their roles, the Winthropians will then meet with the student who has previously been assigned the role of Winthrop; the Hutchinsonians will also meet at a place announced by the Gamemaster. The immigrants and John Cotton will meet with the Gamemaster.

The Winthropians will decide whom they wish to propose for election as Pastor of the Boston Church; they will also select someone who will serve as Deputy Governor and preside over the General Court in Winthrop's absence. The Friends of Anne will elect a "First Friend of Anne" and also propose someone for election as Pastor of the Boston Church. Both groups will return to class ten minutes before it ends.

Then the Gamemaster will supervise an election for someone to serve as Pastor of the Boston Church—and his assistant. The church members will then vote as a whole on these posts. (Immigrants cannot vote; John Cotton can vote but cannot take either of these posts.)

At the end of this class, Governor Winthrop will announce the name of his Deputy Governor.

John Cotton, the Teacher, may meet with either or both factions, or none at all. While the factions are meeting, the instructor will meet first collectively with the immigrants and then individually with them to discuss their roles.

CLASS 3 (PREPARATORY SESSION C)

The class will meet first to discuss basic issues of game organization. But most of this session will be devoted to faction meetings. Governor Winthrop will lead his group, and the Hutchinsonians, if they have not already done so, will meet and select their leader, the "First Friend of Anne."

During faction meetings, each group should discuss who will prepare papers on which topics. Leaders should ensure that some papers or sermons are being presented at EACH session. Another item for discussion will be strategy for interviewing immigrants. Who will ask what types of questions? Factions are also advised to arrange to meet outside of class. This is a complicated game, and teams must meet frequently to make sense of it all.

While the factions are meeting, the instructor will meet with the indeterminates. The indeterminates do NOT form a team. They represent very different types of puritans, and they may be competing with each other—most of them will likely seek admission to the Boston Church (and thus to the General Court); not all are likely to be accepted. Indeterminates should not discuss the details of their roles with each other or with anyone else until they are sure of what they are doing. The instructor may provide some guidance.

CLASS 4: GAME SESSION #1

Setting   **Boston Church**
Opening Sermon by Pastor: On Preparation and Assurance [10 minutes]
Examination of 2 immigrants [30 minutes]
5-minute recess
General Court

Presentations by Friends of Anne (Friends of Hutchinson present initial grounds for retrial)

Boston Church: Sermon and Papers

Sermon: **Pastor**
2 Immigrants will present initial papers, which will be posted on Web site.

This class will open as a meeting of the Boston Church. (If the Pastor wishes, the seating may be arranged in rows, as in church.) The Pastor will open with a reading of Scripture. The Pastor must also give a sermon outlining the orthodox idea of assurance: One's good behavior and piety (sanctification) can lead to a reasonable confidence—assurance—that he or she has been saved.

Afterwards, immigrants are free to petition the congregation for admission as members of the congregation; to this end, they will customarily read a statement indicating their reasons for believing that they are of the elect (i.e., puritan saints) and warrant admission. Anyone may ask whatever questions or offer whatever comments he or she wishes.

The congregation can then vote on whether to admit any immigrant; someone who has been turned down or deferred on one day can apply for admission on the next. But no one may again seek admission on the same day that they have already been turned down or deterred.

General Court

Welcome and Opening Address by **Governor Winthrop** to the General Court
½ **Friends of Anne** will present initial petitions

After the church business has been finished—and Governor Winthrop or the First Friend of Anne is entitled to ask that matters be speeded up—the class will be immediately reconstituted as the General Court. (That is, Governor Winthrop will exchange places with the Pastor.) Massachusetts Bay Colony was not a theocracy: The clergy did not rule the colony. But it was a puritan commonwealth, which meant that the civil agency—the government—worked hand in glove with the orthodox puritan ministry and vice versa. (Orthodox here means those who opposed Wheelwright and Hutchinson.) Thus clergy will speak and vote on the General Court, and Winthrop will speak freely as a member of the Boston congregation. Winthrop will address the General Court. Afterwards, members of the Hutchinsonian faction will present petitions and arguments on why Anne should be acquitted; these early presentations will likely focus on the transcript of the first trial.

CLASS 5: GAME SESSION # 2 (AS ABOVE)

Presentation of remaining immigrant petitions
Remaining sermons, statements, petitions by Friends of Anne
First half of sermons, statements, etc. by Winthropian faction

CLASS 6: GAME SESSION # 3 (AS ABOVE)

Remaining sermons, statements by Winthropian faction
Second statements, petitions, by ½ of Friends of Anne

CLASS 7: GAME SESSION # 4 (AS ABOVE)

Second sermons, statements by ½ of Winthropian faction
Second sermons, statements by final ½ of Friends of Anne

CLASS 8: GAME SESSION # 5 (AS ABOVE)

Immigrant re-petitions allowed
More debate in General Court

CLASS 9: GAME SESSION # 6

Second papers by all remaining members of General Court
Second papers by all immigrants
General Court votes on Anne Hutchinson
Game ends

CLASS 10: POST MORTEM DISCUSSION

The game is over. The instructor will declare the winners and also help uncover elements
of the game that were not clear to all of the players. During the last half of the final
session, students will discard their roles and become themselves again, discussing the
issues from their own point of view.

Game Rules

The Governor and Pastor are obliged to allow **all persons to present petitions** or to
address the General Court and the church assembly, subject to the constraints the
Governor and the Pastor deem suitable to ensure orderly and reasonable discussion.
However, the Gamemaster may modify these and any other rules.

Although all inhabitants of Boston may present petitions and speak, either to the General
Court or the church, not all may VOTE in those bodies. All decisions of the **church
congregation** are taken by **majority vote, but only church members are entitled to
vote in congregational matters**. (In fact, the churches tried to work by consensus of

church members.) The congregation has the power to dismiss the Pastor and name a new one.

All decisions of the **General Court are also taken by majority vote**. But not everyone is entitled to vote; the voting members of the General Court include all of those who were free male settlers at the outset of the game and, among the recent arrivals to Boston, only the male settlers who have been admitted as members to the Boston Church.

An immigrant who is not a church member does not have a vote in the government of the colony. Most immigrants will petition the church for admission; usually the petition will explain why they believe they warrant consideration as saints in the puritan church. (Recall: The Boston congregation will only admit those who have presented credible evidence of their salvation.) The church may interrogate the applicant and defer action as it sees fit. The church congregation decides all matters, including admission of new members, by majority vote. (This marks a departure from the historical situation, but there are good reasons for it.) Illustrative conversion narratives are included in the appendix.

The General Court cannot replace Governor Winthrop, whose term of office does not expire for some time.

ORAL PRESENTATIONS

You can participate freely in all oral discussions, whether in the General Court or the Boston Church. Even non-members of the Church and Court may address those bodies. Governor Winthrop will preside over the General Court, and the Pastor, over the Boston Church. They will determine who can speak and when, though with due regard, doubtless, of the need for a full airing of views. Additionally, each class will have a podium, at which anyone may stand, thereby claiming an absolute right to give a speech, a sermon, or otherwise ask and address questions. If someone is already at the podium, you may form a line behind her. There is one constraint on speeches: While you may bring notes to the podium or refer to them in remarks from your seat, you may not **read** your speech. If the exact form of your words is important to you, you should write out your speech and publish it. Your written work, with certain exceptions, must somehow be distributed to the people of Boston (photocopies, Web site). Speeches, comments, or questions may also be offered without going to the podium: But again, while reference to notes is allowed, no one may read aloud verbatim text. The Gamemaster will interrupt those who do so.

DISCLOSURE REQUIREMENT

For sessions of the General Court or the Boston Church, all public presentations must be submitted to the entire community. (In point of historical fact, some candidates for church membership—women especially—could request that they not present their narrative to the entire membership, but instead do so privately to a delegation of church elders.)

SECRECY CONCERNING YOUR ROLE

In life, most people are assigned multiple roles whose scripts conflict. We are never sure exactly how to sort them out, and thus we never really know our ultimate goals. Most of us perform as students, parents, spouses, employees, Republicans, Democrats, etc., without being fully conscious of our goals, or, more precisely, without understanding how one role may alter our performance of another. (One example: Bosses may script a role that requires our total commitment to work, and they may offer us abundant and tangible rewards for a good performance; yet we may sometimes reject this role because our friends or family demand a very different performance.) Few know their own ultimate goals, and others who presume to know that information about us deceive themselves.

For this reason, and for some practical ones as well, no player may show his or her "role page" to anyone else. If any player does disclose this information, you should be suspicious. The Gamemaster has likely sent them an alternative role via e-mail. All players are free, as in life, to affirm verbally what they are about: to indicate their goals. And, as in life, all auditors may or may not choose to believe what they hear.

ASSIGNMENTS AND GRADES

Written Assignments

For this game, everyone should plan on submitting at least two papers. (Cotton is an exception.) If you are a member of the Anti-Hutchinson or Pro-Hutchinson factions, your papers may consist of sermons, petitions, prayers, Biblical exegesis, rebuttals, personal denunciations, etc. If you are in the Anti-Hutchinson faction, you should work with Governor Winthrop or the orthodox clergy. If you are in the Pro-Hutchinson faction, you should work with the First Friend of Anne. If you are an immigrant, you may submit any of the above documents, but additionally, you may choose to submit a biographical statement as part of your application for church admission; you may work alone on this or choose to approach anyone else in the community. If you are John Cotton, the Teacher, you should work alone: You should not join a faction ever, though in the last session you are obliged to side with one or the other.

Working As a Team

If you are working with a faction, the faction should cooperatively decide to apportion the workload. Remember: It is far more effective to subdivide your argument into components, and have each person specialize, rather than have everyone write a broad (and thin) essay on the main issue. For example, it would be wasteful for each member of the Winthrop/orthodox minister group to write an essay/speech: "Why Anne Hutchinson Should Be Convicted." A far more effective strategy would be for one person to write an essay on "Anne Hutchinson Demeans Our Ministers" and another on "Hutchinson's Views Will Destroy Our Community" and another on "Hutchinson's Assurance Is Likely the Work of the Devil." Similarly, the defenders of Mrs. Hutchinson might apportion the work in essays such as: "Is God's Grace Something Weak?" or

"Governor Winthrop Is Becoming Like Charles I of England" or "Why Do the Orthodox Ministers Doubt Mrs. Hutchinson's Revelations?"

Grades

Each instructor will determine the relationship between written work and oral presentations and also how much of a "victory" bonus winning teams will receive.

Historical Background

JUDAISM AND THE ORIGINS OF MONOTHEISM

In the fifth century B.C., Athenians commenced their Assembly meetings with the sacrifice of a pig. This was to ensure that the gods look upon their deliberations with favor. **Pagan theology** was complicated. How did anyone know which god they should pray to? And if one god favored Athens and another Corinth, which god would prevail in a contest between the two? If the gods were capricious and fundamentally human in their attributes, how could they be trusted? Pagan cosmology did not provide a very restrictive or coherent guide to behavior and morality.

Perhaps fifteen hundred years earlier, another religion—**Judaism**—was developing along different lines: monotheism, the belief in a single god. This deity was no mysterious spirit or essence of nature, but a god who possessed fundamental human traits. He occasionally intervened in the affairs of mortals, as did the Greek gods and goddesses, but the deity of the Israelites was more foreboding and remote. He was unrivaled by other gods: His name was ineffable. He set down laws and commanded human beings to obey them. On the other hand, this deity had selected some human beings for special treatment: He had chosen the Israelites as "a kingdom of priests and a holy nation" to be an exemplar for mankind. In return for their special treatment, the Israelites were obliged by God to obey special laws, the Ten Commandments; those who failed to do so could expect divine retribution. God told the prophet Amos: "You only have I known of all the families of the earth; therefore I will punish you for all your iniquities." The Israelites were keenly attuned to determining the wishes and expectations of this deity. Their prophets and priests, rabbinical sages and philosophers puzzled over the meaning of the words of the sacred books. How were people to interpret these august words and best adhere to His laws and expectations?

THE RISE OF CHRISTIANITY

Christianity grew out of this monotheistic tradition. The Christian savior—Jesus Christ—was himself a Jew. Christ accepted the Judaic law but placed new and special emphasis on a passage in Leviticus 19:18—"love thy neighbor as thyself." This became, in fact, one of Christ's new injunctions, or laws. His disciples came to regard him not as merely another Hebrew prophet, but as an extension of God, a "son" of God. Christ was crucified, and his followers saw him restored from the dead—proof, they claimed, of his divinity. The Christians added a second volume to the Hebrew sacred writings; this New Testament reflected God's additional words since the advent of Christ. The Christians assumed that the two books were related: The Old Testament anticipated, or prefigured, the coming of Christ, chronicled in the New Testament. Together, the volumes constituted the Bible. [A more detailed "road map" of the Bible is included later in this booklet.] Christian scholars, like the most learned minds of the Israelites, scoured this sacred volume to understand what God wanted of them.

Christianity spread, especially among the poorer peoples of the Mediterranean basin. A wide diversity of beliefs sprang up under its umbrella. It also slowly acquired a hierarchical institutional structure that evolved into the papacy: a single church leader, following in the footsteps of Christ and Peter, who was called as the "rock" of the Christian church; his office became institutionalized as the papacy, with Peter regarded, in the Catholic tradition, as the first pope. The diffusion of Christianity was facilitated by the conversion of the Roman Emperor Constantine (306 to 337 A.D.). Constantine made Christianity legal in 313 A.D., and in 380 A.D., it became the official religion of the Roman Empire. As soon as Christians had access to the power of the state, they began persecuting each other.

After the fall of Rome, and during the subsequent period of lawlessness, Christian practices and precepts were perpetuated in remote monasteries, where theologians wrestled over abstruse points of doctrine, sometimes contending with the papacy. With the gradual restoration of order after 1100 AD, the Christian Church worked with (though often against) the various kings and queens of the states of Western Europe. The revival of trade and the growth of towns and cities strengthened the economic foundations of the church and increased its power. By the 1400s the pope in Rome was head of what was arguably the most powerful institution in Europe: the Roman Catholic Church.

MARTIN LUTHER AND THE PROTESTANT REFORMATION

The Protestant Reformation began in the early 1500s as a reaction to the maturation and bureaucratization of the Roman Catholic Church. Catholic reformers such as Martin Luther (1483-1546) were shocked by what they perceived as the spiritual laxity of the Church hierarchy: the sale of church offices to the highest bidder and the widespread sale of indulgences (forgiveness of sin); the sexual promiscuity of popes and priests; and the Church's entanglement in landed estates and commercial affairs.

The reformers regarded the institutional corruption of the Church as merely the outward expression of a deeper moral rot and doctrinal perversion: They maintained that the Catholic Church paid for its institutional expansion by offering deals to those seeking salvation. Protestant reformers rejected much of the ritual and theology of the Church, arguing that these had gone far astray from what they thought the Bible dictated. They strove to minimize the roles of human intermediaries between man and God, thus eliminating many of the occasions for corruption. The failure of the Catholic hierarchy to respond to the reformers' complaints caused them to break from the Catholic Church. They did so claiming that it was a false church and under the dominion of **Antichrist**, a satanic being who was the embodiment of evil and the most cunning opponent of true Christianity.

Luther envisioned a reformation of religion, not a restructuring of society. But other reformers in Germany read far more radical lessons from the Bible. They started questioning private property, the rule of governments, and even the sanctity of marriage. Many of them believed that God sent them personal revelations. They thought that both the Bible and common sense showed that baptism could be offered only to adults who understood what it meant, which is why they went under the blanket term of Anabaptists. The most notorious Anabaptists seized the city of Münster in 1534. Guided by the revelations of their leader, John of Leiden, they murdered anyone who disagreed with them, banned money, and practiced forced polygamy (John had sixteen wives). They were bloodily repressed, and the Anabaptists of Münster became a byword among Protestants for the dangers of radical Protestantism, revelations, and unguided Bible interpretation. Their long shadow stretched even over Massachusetts a hundred years later, in part because a group called the **Family of Love** preserved and elaborated on many of their ideas. **Familists** were active in England, although illegal, and we know that a number of the colonists and ministers encountered them.

THE PROTESTANT REFORMATION IN ENGLAND

The Protestant Reformation arrived in England under complicated circumstances. Luther's ideas began slipping into England around the same time that King Henry VIII (1491-1547) started seeking a divorce in the 1520s. When the Pope refused to annul his marriage, Henry rejected the Pope and the Catholic Church. Along the way, he confiscated much of the church's property for the crown. Henry was not interested in reforming the church, beyond putting himself in control of it, but out of necessity he had to rely on more committed reformers for support. Henry's young son Edward (1537-1553), on the other hand, was a devoted Protestant to the end of his short life. Edward's successor and half-sister, the Catholic Mary (1516-1558) made the country Catholic again. She was unable to root out Protestantism in her brief reign, however, despite burning nearly three hundred Protestants and driving many more into exile.

Mary's successor, her half-sister Elizabeth (1533-1603), guided the Act of Supremacy through Parliament in 1559, which made the Church of England Protestant once more and Elizabeth its head. But Elizabeth was an extremely conservative Protestant. Many of her subjects thought that she did not go far enough to cleanse the church of its Catholic rites and its hierarchical government by bishops and archbishops. Nor, they felt, was there enough provision to insure that the church had ministers capable of saving souls by their powerful preaching. Those critics were called by their opponents "puritans."

Puritanism was a loose movement of Protestant piety, protest, and reform. Moderate puritans were mainly concerned with providing zealous preachers in each of England's parishes and permeating English society with their severe moral code. Less compromising puritans refused to conform to the elements in the Church of England they regarded as sinful, non-biblical, and too Catholic. They wished to smash all the remaining stained glass windows and statues of God and the saints in the churches as invitations to idol worship. The Church's official prayer book, they felt, too closely conformed to the Catholic missal, which outlined the prayers and responses for the Catholic mass; the Church of England's priestly garments resembled those of the Catholic priests; and the practice of kneeling at the sacrament of the Lord's Supper violated biblical practice (Jesus's disciples sat when He gave them His last supper), among other issues. The most radical puritans wanted to go even further. They would remodel the government of the Church of England according to what they thought was the Bible's simple, consensual pattern. They would eliminate bishops, who were appointed by the monarch, and who in turn appointed each parish's minister and supervised its affairs. Instead, each congregation would elect its own ministers and mostly run its own affairs in a system called presbyterianism. Puritan nonconformists ran the risk of being pulled into ecclesiastical and royal courts, where they faced fines, imprisonment, and the loss of their ministry.

As they attempted to change the church, puritans pursued an intense religious life of their own. They traveled many miles to hear their favorite preachers, and they met in private, semi-legal groups (**conventicles**). In those groups, they recounted their personal religious struggles, studied the Bible and their favorite sermons, discussed the state of the Church of England, and prayed for change in the Church.

In order to change the Church legally, puritans worked through Parliament, which was sympathetic to them. Elizabeth blocked all efforts at parliamentary reform, and frustrated puritans were at the forefront of efforts to assert the rights and liberties of parliament against her. Elizabeth was succeeded by James I (1566-1625), also the king of Scotland, in 1603. Scotland was presbyterian—exactly what the most radical English puritans wanted—and puritans had high hopes for reform when James took the throne. But in the 1590s, James had engaged in protracted political battles with the Scottish presbyterians. From those battles, he concluded that presbyterianism was too democratic for kings. The more authoritarian, crown-appointed government of the Church of England suited monarchs much better. "No bishops, no king" was his famous saying. When he became James I of England in 1603, he dashed the hopes of the puritans; there would be no changes in the church.

In James' reign, the struggles between parliament and the crown spread beyond the issue of puritanism. James resorted to extra-legal means to raise money for his depleted treasury and raised concerns about the liberties of parliament and of Englishmen in doing so—the future battle cry of the American Revolution, no taxation without representation, had old English roots, and that cry was raised more forcefully under James than ever before. To the further alarm of most of his subjects, James grew increasingly lenient toward Catholics, in part because the only available brides of noble enough birth for his son Charles (1600-1649) were from Catholic France and Spain.

James died in 1625. Charles I proved an even more authoritarian ruler. He focused far more than his father on crushing puritanism, and he had little love for parliament, which responded to him and his requests, he felt, with insufficient obedience. He married a French Catholic princess in 1625 and coerced money from his subjects in 1627 (the Forced Loan). Puritans rapidly began to see a sinister conspiracy at work behind Charles' agenda, in which Catholic agents (and thus the agents of Antichrist) were attempting to exterminate both Protestantism and English liberties. In response, radical puritans began planning the Massachusetts Bay Colony as a puritan refuge in 1627, where puritans could finally create the kind of churches that they believed the Bible called for and form a morally upright society. Note that they were not planning to leave because they sought religious freedom; they were planning to leave because England's rulers were failing in their sacred obligation to follow God's will.

In 1629, these puritans applied for a charter from the English crown. The charter would make them a legal corporation and grant them land in North America that Charles claimed to own. Charles I was not disposed to do any favors for the puritans, but he was eager to strengthen British claims in the New World. And he doubtless concluded that the emigration of thousands of troublesome puritans from England and into the forests of the Americas would not be an altogether bad thing. So the crown granted the charter. By the terms of the charter, a General Court (or meeting) of the company's shareholders made the company's regulations and laws, while a Governor and a much smaller Court of Assistants acted as the planning and executive board for the company (in Massachusetts, the governor and assistants were also called magistrates). Now the planning of the settlement of Massachusetts Bay depended on the leadership of a small group of English puritans. Foremost among them was John Winthrop.

JOHN WINTHROP AND THE ORIGINS OF THE MASSACHUSETTS BAY COLONY

John Winthrop (1588-1649) came from a third-generation puritan family. His grandfather Adam Winthrop, a London cloth merchant, bought a monastery in rural Suffolk in 1546 from King Henry VIII that the king had confiscated from the Catholic Church. Adam then set himself up as a country gentleman, the Lord of Groton Manor, and John Winthrop inherited his title. By the time of John's birth, Suffolk was one of the most deeply puritan regions of England. The puritan ideal there, however imperfectly realized, of rulers and ministers working together to shape a model Christian society would provide the foundation for his vision of Massachusetts. At fifteen he entered Cambridge University and began to consider becoming a minister, but he left after two years. At eighteen he married and turned to the practice of law to make a living.

In the 1620s, Winthrop, like puritans in general, worried deeply about the state of England. English kings grew increasingly hostile to the liberties of the English people, and the leaders of the Church of England grew increasingly hostile to puritanism. Meanwhile, society grew increasingly corrupt, Winthrop felt, and the country became mired in economic hard times. He tried and failed to get elected to the Parliament of 1624 (a draft of a bill he wrote against drunkenness survives). As his family grew, his finances steadily worsened, and in 1627, he left his family to live most of the year in London, where he served as a lawyer handling routine business at the Court of Wards—an obscure branch of the judicial system that dealt with the inherited assets of minors. By the end of that decade, Winthrop was a middle-aged man whose career as a lawyer had stalled and whose modest wealth was in decline. He was in his third marriage; his first two wives had died, and Winthrop had twelve children, the oldest of whom were in their twenties.

Winthrop was well connected and respected among leading puritans, and he became actively involved in the planning of the Massachusetts Bay colony, an effort to create a refuge for puritans in New England. After receiving its royal charter in 1629, the Massachusetts Bay Company faced the formidable problem of getting a proper leadership across the Atlantic. Puritans had been trying to settle New England for most of the 1620s. But so far, the region had proven a sinkhole for money, while colonies in their early years were notorious for their high mortality rates.

The situation in England grew still grimmer for puritans in 1629. King Charles had dissolved Parliament, guardian of English liberty, in March, and it was widely expected that he would try hard never to have to call one again. He appointed William Laud, untiring foe of puritans, to be bishop of London. Winthrop and some other shareholders in the Massachusetts Bay Company met in June and came up with a bold plan. They agreed that they would cross the Atlantic themselves, but only if their fellow freemen of the company elected them to be the company's new government and they could take the charter with them. With the government and charter of the company in Massachusetts, the colony would be in practice a puritan self-governing commonwealth.

Winthrop possessed considerable as-yet-unutilized leadership skills and an unbending devotion to the cause of the colony, and thus he was a logical person to be elected to the thankless position of governor to lead the migration to Massachusetts in 1630. In addition to arranging for supplies and contracting for the ships, Winthrop recruited puritans for the expedition and wrote arguments in favor of settlement, distributing them to prominent puritans. He helped find sponsors for those who could not pay their own way. He also reassured investors in the Massachusetts Bay Company that the enterprise would be well run. (In fact, the enterprise never proved financially profitable.)

In March 1630 a flotilla of four ships and 400 emigrants gathered in Southampton harbor, the beginning of a migration of nearly 1,000 people that year. Winthrop preached a famous sermon to the group—whether onboard the flagship *Arbella* or on land is not known—entitled "A Model of Christian Charity" (portions of that sermon are included in the "Primary Documents" section of the appendix). In it, he outlined his vision of their future colony. They were fleeing England in order to worship God correctly, so they had a special commission from Him. If He brought them to America safely, that meant that He expected them to create an ideal Christian society. There would be rich and poor, rulers and ruled. But everyone would act toward each other with selfless, Christian love and bear each other's burdens. The rich would freely give to the poor and forgive their debts if the poor could not repay. In times of the colony's need, everyone would have to be prepared to sacrifice all that they had. If they did so, God would bless them and they would prosper. Invoking a Scripture passage popular among puritan ministers (Matthew 5: 14-16), Winthrop warned listeners that they would be like a city on a hill and that the eyes of all people would be on them. If they succeeded, people would say of future colonies, "The Lord make it like that of New England." If they followed selfish goals, God would destroy them, and their failure would give ammunition to the enemies of puritanism.

THE DIFFICULT FIRST YEAR IN MASSACHUSETTS, 1630-1631

After a two-month voyage across the North Atlantic, the flotilla sighted the New England coast. After briefly stopping at Salem, Winthrop moved the entire expedition to the broad bay at the mouth of the Charles River; tiny groups of emigrants spread out and settled in Charlestown, Boston, Dorchester, Roxbury, Watertown, and Newtown (Cambridge). Winthrop himself remained in Boston, which soon became the economic and political center of the colony.

Although they arrived in the summer, food was scarce. Many of the provisions had rotted on the long journey over, and the settlers did not know how to hunt the plentiful native game. Winthrop dispatched sailors in small boats to trade with the Indians for corn, which he then distributed among the neediest settlers. Many people waded into the bay at low tide searching for mussels to eat. Meanwhile, some settlers pitched tents; others began to fashion rude habitations from logs and mud. Winthrop and a few others built frame homes from planks produced from a sawmill.

That winter was fiercer than anything they had experienced in England. Many suffered from frostbite; some froze to death when caught in sudden snowstorms. By February, many were starving. Of the roughly thousand immigrants who arrived in Massachusetts Bay Colony in 1630, about two hundred died; another two hundred returned to England the following spring. Among the dead were eleven of Winthrop's own servants. Yet Winthrop kept up his determination and faith that God intended their endeavor to succeed. He threw himself bodily into the colony's survival, literally, doing manual labor to encourage others. In the first dreadful winter he fed the colonists out of his personal supplies, and thereafter when necessary he paid for public expenses out of his own pocket. Winthrop confined himself almost entirely to water as his drink and kept his meals simple in order to serve as a model of sobriety and self-restraint for the rest of the colonists. In February 1631, while others were resolving to abandon New England, Winthrop sent word to his wife, who had remained in England with the children, to join him on the next possible sailing.

THE GROWTH OF THE COLONY AFTER 1631

Winthrop's leadership was essential, but what ultimately saved Massachusetts Bay Colony was a flood of immigrants after 1633. They brought money, food, tools, clothing, and skills. The colony's deliverance, ironically, had been caused by a man many of them regarded as their greatest enemy: William Laud, whom King Charles I appointed in 1633 as Achbishop of Canterbury, the leader of the Church of England. In England, Laud resolved to stamp out puritan influence in the church. He purged puritan ministers and insisted that all parishes obey all of the rituals of the Church of England, some of which had never been previously enforced. Puritan critics denounced him. Laud's insistence on impressive vestments, expensive altar implements, and showy rites, the critics insisted, implied that God could be influenced by such shows. Laud horrified them by reintroducing stained glass windows and religious statues in churches—idol worship, charged the puritans, who had destroyed almost all the medieval stained glass and statues in English churches. Laud, they claimed, was abandoning the fundamental principles of the Protestant Reformation. Puritans suggested that Laud secretly intended to reunite the Church of England with the Catholic Church, at a time when Catholic monarchs were engaged in a devastating war against the Protestants of Germany. Many puritans responded by fleeing to Massachusetts.

One of these was John Cotton (1584-1652), a prominent nonconformist minister in Lincolnshire, England. In 1633 he emigrated to Massachusetts Bay Colony after he had received a summons to appear before one of Laud's courts. Cotton, one of the most famous puritans, was immediately elected Teacher of the Boston Church, the minister responsible for guidance on theological matters. Soon after Cotton arrived, the churches in Massachusetts started an important innovation in puritan practice. Massachusetts churches, following the example of the radical puritan presbyterians, already required that all who sought membership in a congregation lead upright lives and make a profession of their beliefs. Now they were to tell the congregation the story of how they came to believe that God had "elected" them to become among His saints and guaranteed that they would be saved and go to heaven. They were to explain specifically what had happened in their life to give them assurance of salvation. The men in the church would then vote on whether the petitioners' narratives were persuasive; if there were no objections, the newcomers would become members of the church.

In Massachusetts Bay Colony, the demand for food, clothing, and tools greatly outpaced supply. As early as August 1630 Winthrop and the General Court set the maximum wages for carpenters, sawyers, and bricklayers at two shillings a day, considerably more than was paid for the same work in England. Later the General Court avoided runaway inflation by fixing the price of English goods at no more than fourpence above what they would have cost in England. Wage and price controls were extremely difficult to enforce and were mostly ignored, but throughout the 1630s Winthrop and other leaders kept introducing legislation that would guide the economy by loftier principles than mere self-interest.

No less importantly, the government saw to it that all the settlers conducted themselves in what it considered a morally upright manner. Everyone was required to attend church. Opponents of the new order were banished, one of them after having his ears cut off for his criticisms of church and state. In the first four years of the colony's existence, the government banned the consumption of tobacco, instituted the death penalty for adultery (with the same penalty for males as females, a radical innovation), and protected the holiness of Sunday (the Sabbath) by giving exceptionally large fines for Sunday drunkenness and by whipping people for shooting birds on that day. It instructed town constables to report all idle people to it, and it forbade what it considered unnecessarily fashionable clothing as a waste of money and as "pernicious to the commonwealth." These kinds of measures were not unheard of elsewhere, but in Massachusetts they were distinguished by their extent and the seriousness with which they were enforced.

As starvation receded as a threat, religious disputes became more frequent.

THE THREAT OF CHARTER REVOCATION, 1634

Meanwhile, King Charles' officials in London were becoming alarmed by the increasingly explicit puritan character of the Massachusetts Bay Colony. In 1634 a ship arrived in Boston carrying a letter indicating that King Charles I had formed a Royal Commission for Regulating Plantations to control all English colonies—including Massachusetts Bay Colony. Worse, the commission was to be headed by Archbishop Laud! Rumors circulated that a British fleet would install a new governor and dismantle the puritan commonwealth. The General Court made plans to recruit a militia in the event of an attack by the British; at the same time, too, war was stirring with the Pequot Indians of southern Connecticut.

In this context, the theological disputes grew more acrimonious. In these, Governor Winthrop was as interested in finding practical solutions as he was in defending narrow ideological positions. He was widely admired for his rectitude, good judgment, and devotion to the colony. However, his regime inevitably built up resentments. Winthrop's leniency with wrongdoers aroused complaints among the severer puritans in the colony. More seriously, he had an authoritarian streak. He refused to bind his behavior to procedural norms and resisted efforts to provide a law code for the colony (he preferred to decide out of his own sense of right and wrong what constituted crimes and what were appropriate sentences). In 1634, as governor he tried in vain to stall when the freemen (voters) demanded the full legislative powers allowed them in the charter. That year, he was voted out of the governor's position.

THE GENERAL COURT BANISHES ROGER WILLIAMS, 1635

Winthrop's leniency, exceptional alertness to the colony's welfare, and tendency to ignore procedural norms all came into play in his intervention in the case of the famous dissenter Roger Williams. Winthrop originally greeted the arrival of Williams, a "godly minister," with enthusiasm. The Boston Church proposed that Williams officiate at its services. But though young Williams was likeable and charismatic, his definition of religious purity was rigid. He declined the offer to lead the Boston Church because it had refused to break formally with the Church of England: "I durst not officiate to an unseparated people," he told them. Over the next few years his demands for religious purity escalated. His initial insistence that the puritans of Massachusetts repent of ever having so much as worshipped in English churches would have been a disaster both for the colony's relationship with the English government and with English puritans, who still worshipped in those churches. To that demand, he added another: that men should not take the oath of loyalty the Massachusetts government demanded of its adult males because taking oaths was sinful. On top of this, he decided that the king had no right to give Massachusetts its land, because it belonged to the Indians, not to the king, and he agitated to have the charter sent back to England.

What made Williams even more dangerous was that he was extremely popular in the town of Salem, which chose him as the minister of its church in early 1635. He threatened to turn the Salem church against the rest of the colony. The colony's ministers tried repeatedly to persuade Williams that he was wrong; the General Court tried to pressure Salem by withholding land from it. When all else failed, the General Court, which by the terms of its royal charter had the right to banish colonists simply if they were an "annoyance," ordered that Williams be sent back to England at the end of 1635.

Winthrop, a Court member, secretly tipped Williams off, and Williams instead fled to what would become Rhode Island. Winthrop, of course, had no business undermining a Court order, but he did so for two reasons. The first was that he did not want to see such a sincere, if misguided, puritan shipped back to a country increasingly hostile to puritanism. The second was that Winthrop correctly surmised that it would be to the long-term benefit of the colony to have a set of eyes and ears in the Indian country to the south of them. Williams stayed on good terms with Winthrop and kept up an important correspondence with him about conditions in his place of exile.

WAR WITH THE PEQUOT INDIANS

For a time the puritans got on fairly well with the Pequot Indians. But as the flow of English immigrants swelled after 1633 and they began pushing farther inland, relations deteriorated. The Pequots were themselves blocked by migration by the Mohegans to the west and the Narragansetts to the south. An incident in the summer of 1636 led to open hostilities. A Boston trader was murdered on Block Island, south of Narragansett Bay

(Rhode Island). The General Court dispatched a military expedition to punish the Pequots, who were thought to be responsible for the trader's death. Pequot crops were destroyed and villages burned; the Pequots, in retaliation, raided some puritan villages.

Captain John Mason, aided by Mohegan and Narragansett Indians, led another expedition that surprised the Pequots at their fort near Mystic, Connecticut, in May 1637. Some 500 or 600 Indian warriors and their families were slaughtered. Many of the defeated Pequots were sold into slavery, and the Mohegans occupied much of the land formerly occupied by the Pequots.

BEGINNINGS OF THE CRISIS WITH ANNE HUTCHINSON, 1636

In 1636 Williams's disaffection was followed by a more momentous theological challenge to orthodoxy in Massachusetts Bay Colony. Only men could hold formal positions of authority, political and religious, in puritan New England. Yet a critical figure in the drama that rocked the foundations of the Massachusetts Bay Colony was a "nimble-tongued" woman: Anne Hutchinson.

Anne Hutchinson

Anne Marbury Hutchinson (1591-1643) was born in the small market town of Alford, Lincolnshire, in England. Her father was a fiery puritan minister, and her mother came from a prominent puritan family. Her childhood home life would have included extensive daily prayer and Bible reading. Anne's mother trained Anne in the arts of nursing, supervising servants, running a household, and looking after a fast-increasing number of younger brothers and sisters. Her mother, too, probably taught her how to read and write.

In 1612, Anne married William Hutchinson, five years older, a puritan and cloth merchant from Alford (historians have argued long and inconclusively about whether specific social groups found puritanism especially attractive). Anne's first child came ten months later, and she was to give birth every year or two until 1633; she had fifteen children. This number was not uncommon, but what was uncommon was that only three of Hutchinson's children died in childhood— at this time over half the population died before reaching the age of three, while 20% of mothers died in childbirth. Hutchinson must have had a strong constitution to match the force of her personality, and her subsequent reputation as a healer seems well founded.

In England, Anne lived about twenty miles away from John Cotton. She admired his preaching immensely, especially his emphasis on experiencing the divine, and she regarded any minister who taught differently than he as dangerously deluded. She knew the Bible in great detail and regarded Bible verses that came into her mind as revelations from God, giving her spiritual insights and even glimpses into the future. She was unusual in the extremely heavy emphasis that she placed on these revelations.

In 1634, Anne and her family boarded the *Griffin* and set sail for Boston. The voyage was a difficult one, and she and her family were "many a week within six inches of Death to see Christ." The Boston Church soon became a hotbed of puritan zeal.

The Hutchinsons quickly fit into their new community. Anne's husband William served as a deputy to the General Court, town selectman, and deacon of the church. The community greatly valued Anne, in part for her help at childbirths and in part because of her ability to lead people to what her ministers regarded as genuine conversions.

They were among the town's wealthiest inhabitants.

Often people came to Anne for advice as to their spiritual state. She told many of them that they relied excessively on their good works—their regular attendance at church, their acts of charity, and their conscious effort to lead a godly life—to prove to themselves that God had saved, or justified, them. This was an error, she told them. Only Christ's free and unbidden gift of grace could save them, and nothing they might do on their own would influence His actions. Some other people, though, described experiences that she found to be far more credible evidence of their justification. These proofs emerged not from that person's thoughts or actions, but from a source external to them—from God—such as God's revealing his decision by causing a fortuitous passage of Scripture to pop into their head and causing a sudden and intense feeling of love and joy permeating their very being. People who had experiences such as these, she assured those who listened to her, had likely been "sealed" to Christ and had thus become one of His Saints. Men as well as women flocked to Hutchinson for advice. Powerfully self-confident, Hutchinson claimed that if she had a half hour's talk with a man, she would be able to tell if he were among the saved or not.

Puritans who had already been elected members of the puritan churches of Massachusetts Bay Colony but had had no recollection of a revelation or an infusion of godly joy found Hutchinson's frank opinions to be both alarming and presumptuous. On the other hand, many other puritans—especially those who had had such experiences and conviction—found her words to be exhilarating and powerful.

Hutchinson began to hold regular meetings in her house, one for women only that she led, and another meeting of men and women. These meetings were notable both for some bold theological speculation and the criticisms that Hutchinson encouraged of most of the colony's ministers. As the crisis in the colony mounted, anger over her meetings rose with it.

Although Hutchinson criticized most of the ministers, there was one in particular whom she idolized. He was John Cotton, Teacher of the Boston Church and doubtless the most respected puritan theologian in the New World. The ministers whom Hutchinson criticized increasingly looked to Cotton for clarification and guidance. Did he approve of the views of his outspoken and devoted follower? Or was he perhaps the source of her opinions?

John Cotton

John Cotton (1585-1652) was a famous scholar and a tireless and much-sought-after counselor to both English and continental Protestants. To his piety and learning Cotton added a mild, nonconfrontational personality. He became a committed puritan nonconformist a few years after taking up his ministry in 1612 in the Lincolnshire port of Boston. His arrival in Massachusetts in 1633 was a great morale boost for the colony. Cotton quickly became Massachusetts' leading minister, although his effort in 1636 to give the colony a legal code closely modeled after the Old Testament was rejected.

Cotton's preaching was in general less harsh and less focused on sin than some ministers'. He seems to have worked out of an intuitive sense of communion with God, and he sometimes expressed his misty theological ideas with hairsplitting details and distinctions that left more conventional listeners uneasily uncertain about what he was really saying. Hutchinson especially admired the way in which Cotton stressed that it was only by experiencing God's love that people could have assurance that they were saved.

Cotton may have formulated his distinctive ideas about assurance of salvation as early as c.1630. When Anne Hutchinson and others began amplifying his differences with the other ministers in early 1636, some ministers attacked him. As they did so, his sympathy rose for Hutchinson and her circle.

HENRY VANE AND JOHN WHEELWRIGHT JOIN THE DISPUTE, 1635-1636

In November 1635, Henry Vane, whose father was one of Charles I's chief advisors, arrived and joined the Boston Church. Although his father was tied to King Charles, Henry Vane greatly admired Hutchinson's spiritual abilities, and he encouraged her to set up well-attended conventicles in which she expounded on Cotton's ideas. While fervently endorsing Cotton's teachings, she, Vane, and others also cautiously, speculatively, and secretively started to add to those ideas other radical notions that some regarded as akin to familism. They also started to criticize the colony's other ministers for failing to preach like Cotton.

Vane was elected governor in May 1636, and that same month Anne Hutchinson's brother-in-law, the minister John Wheelwright, arrived in Massachusetts Bay Colony and became a member of the Boston Church.

Backed by Vane, Hutchinson and Wheelwright complained that the orthodox ministers of Massachusetts Bay Colony were preaching a doctrine that led toward the corruptions they associated with Roman Catholicism. In their view, the orthodox ministers held that those saints whom God had elected to receive His grace and be saved from damnation might not have any strong sense that they had received that gift—they might not have a sense of **assurance** of their election. Because of that, the ministers instructed such people to seek signs of assurance in their good works—their regular attendance in church, their refraining from sinful behavior, their pious thoughts, and their acts of charity. But this emphasis on their good works, according to Hutchinson and her allies, logically led to the Catholic notion (and thus Antichrist's notion) that good works could persuade God to "save" those who, like all mortals, warranted damnation.

Hutchinson publicly claimed to believe nothing more than Wheelwright and Cotton, and they and their supporters took her at face value. However, as rumors of the radical ideas circulating in Boston spread, along with criticisms of the other ministers, some panicky clergy and other leaders of the colony foresaw the colony heading into a situation resembling the anarchy of Münster, driven by the ideas of Hutchinson and her allies. These orthodox clergy turned the spotlight of their concern onto Wheelwright and Cotton. Wheelwright was widely suspected of encouraging heresies about revelations and union with God, while some ministers attacked Cotton's own teaching as being fundamentally wrong and as lying at the heart of the problem. As Cotton and Wheelwright came under attack, they in turn criticized the orthodox ministers for teaching false doctrine; the two also refused to acknowledge anything seriously amiss in the Boston congregation.

In October 1636 Cotton, Hutchinson, and Wheelwright met with eight other ministers to explain themselves. The ministers finally concluded that Cotton and Wheelwright "gave satisfaction," but mutual suspicions quickly flared back up. Hutchinson's answers at this meeting eventually led to charges of slandering the ministers and her trial a year later. The dispute seriously weakened the colony, already suspect among English puritans for its radically democratic presbyterian-inspired form of church government and under the threat of having its royal charter revoked by Charles I's government. Through 1636, the General Court stayed out of the dispute, in part because it was usually not supposed to interfere in church matters and in part because there were important people on both sides of this quarrel.

FAST DAY, JANUARY 1637

As tensions in the colony mounted, the General Court proclaimed a day of fasting and prayer on January 19, 1637. Wheelwright was invited to give a sermon at the event, and he responded by fanning the flames of discord. He began by denouncing the notion of the "fast day" itself as further evidence of Massachusetts' descent toward Popery and Antichrist. "Many tymes those that are the least acquainted with the Lord Jesus are given the most of all to fasting, the Papists are given much to fasting and punish themselves by whipping," he declared. Without naming his opponents (the orthodox ministers), he denounced them as foes of Jesus and called for a spiritual combat in the colony, whatever the cost. The orthodox ministers gave some fiery sermons of their own. Wheelwright ended up on trial before the General Court in March 1637. He was convicted of sedition (language or conduct that could incite a disturbance against legal authority) because of the fast-day sermon. The three-day trial was a close one, and the hostile intervention of the bulk of the colony's ministers determined its outcome.

For Wheelwright's supporters, this outcome was persecution of the Gospel. They sent an angry petition to the General Court denouncing the conviction as unjustified; the Court, they added, was doubtless under the influence of Satan. No English governing body at this time recognized an automatic right of people to criticize its actions, but because powerful men like Vane and Cotton sympathized with the petition, the General Court did not respond for the time being.

The orthodox ministers in turn complained that their views had been misrepresented. Worse, scores of members of the Boston Church were flocking to Hutchinson's house, where Mrs. Hutchinson and her allies were persuading themselves that their own intense emotional responses were proof of God's grace. Some of them went to other churches and challenged the ministers after their sermons. The orthodox ministers feared Hutchinson and her allies would undermine civil and public order and rip apart the bonds of fellowship within the churches.

WINTHROP DEFEATS VANE AS GOVERNOR, MAY 1637

In May, the colony held its critical annual election for governor. John Winthrop, a vocal opponent of Wheelwright and Hutchinson, chose to challenge Henry Vane. The election would constitute a referendum on the theological issues that had embroiled the colony for several years. Winthrop was supported by the orthodox ministers, and Vane by Hutchinson, Wheelwright, and many in the Boston Church.

On election day—May 17, 1637—the freemen of the colony gathered in Newtown (Cambridge) to vote. When it came time to vote, Vane's supporters tried to stall. Those supporting Winthrop walked to one side of the common. Winthrop's group was larger; he was the winner.

But criticism of Winthrop and the ministers persisted. Rumors circulated about a sudden influx of immigrants who might tip the political scales in favor of Hutchinson and the critics. The General Court passed a law holding that no "strangers" could remain in the colony longer than three weeks without its permission.

Unlike some of his supporters, Winthrop took great pains to cultivate John Cotton and try to win him over to his side during the crisis. He did this partially out of his deep admiration for Cotton and partially because he feared that Cotton's departure from the colony would seriously threaten its survival. In no small part thanks to Winthrop's efforts, by the time of Anne Hutchinson's trial, Cotton had come around to an uneasy neutrality.

"THE CHURCHES ARE ON FIRE," SUMMER 1637

Over the summer, the crisis reached a boiling point. "The churches are on fire," fishermen cried to the immigrant ships sailing into Boston harbor. In July, when a boatload of immigrants docked in Boston harbor, including many from Lincolnshire (and a brother of Hutchinson's husband), magistrates interrogated them on their religious views. Those who refused to repudiate Wheelwright's opinions (shared in more extreme form by Mrs. Hutchinson) were given four months to either change their mind or leave the colony. Cotton and most of the Boston congregation were enraged that devout Christians were being turned away. They considered the law a violation of their rights as English people, an affront to the gospel, and even as a manifestation of the tyrannical spirit of Roman Catholicism. In protest, Vane, Cotton, and many others from Boston planned to found another colony that summer. To add to Massachusetts' troubles, its royal charter had been revoked in May.

The colony might have collapsed under the weight of these difficulties. But King Charles and Laud never had a chance to control the puritan experiment in Massachusetts. They were beset with problems in England and Scotland. Their effort to remodel the puritan Church of Scotland drove that land into rebellion in the summer of 1637, and Charles' support in England was too weak for him to launch an effective counteroffensive. The plan by Cotton and Vane to emigrate fell through, for unknown reasons, and Vane returned to England at the beginning of August. At a synod (meeting) of the New England churches held at the end of the summer, Cotton backed off from some of his previous positions and worked out a theological compromise with the other ministers.

WHEELWRIGHT BANISHED, NOVEMBER 1637

Wheelwright, however, refused to assent and was unwilling to leave the colony voluntarily. The General Court ordered that he be banished at the beginning of November, along with another of his supporters. Other supporters of Wheelwright received lesser penalties.

FIRST TRIAL OF ANNE HUTCHINSON

Then the General Court turned to interrogate Mrs. Hutchinson. Her trial represented a greater challenge to Winthrop and his allies than the trial of Wheelwright. Where Wheelwright and his male allies had actively engaged in extremely public expressions of hostility against the ministers and government of Massachusetts, Hutchinson, as a woman, had not, and when Winthrop invited her to defend Wheelwright, she pointedly refused to do so. Winthrop expressed the charges against Hutchinson very unclearly in his opening speech, but her crimes added up to sedition. She was not convicted on all the specific charges. The official Court record gives her contemptuous remarks about the ministers and her warning to the court of divine vengeance against it as the grounds for her conviction. Criticizing an authority figure in church or state at this time was regarded as seditious, even if the criticism was true. When Hutchinson, on the authority of a scriptural Biblical revelation, threatened the Court with divine wrath if it convicted her, that in itself constituted sedition, as well as contempt of court. The Court voted almost unanimously to convict Hutchinson for slandering the ministers and threatening the Court. It sentenced her to be banished in the following spring. Meanwhile, she was put under house arrest.

WAS HUTCHINSON GUILTY?

In debate between Hutchinson, her witnesses, and the ministers about her alleged slander were five questions: 1) Did she say the ministers were under a covenant of works? 2) Did she say they were not able ministers of the New Testament? 3) Did she say that the letter of the Bible teaches a covenant of works? 4) Were these slanderous criticisms? and finally, 5) Whatever criticisms she made of the ministers, did she make them only after a great deal of pressure from the ministers themselves?

The main thrust of Hutchinson's defense was twofold: 1) The ministers had exaggerated what she said about them; and 2) The ministers minimized the degree to which she only spoke at their urging. That defense was based on the fact that the Massachusetts government continually stressed that it did not prosecute people for their beliefs as long as they kept those beliefs to themselves. When ministers, godly advisors, pressed her for her opinions, surely she would be expected to share them. Hutchinson herself made it clear that she had said some very severe things about the ministers, but only in one-on-one conversations that she assumed were private and in which the ministers expected her to be honest. One bone of contention was whether Hutchinson was really having an open conversation with the ministers or whether she was just preaching to them, for there was no automatic legal right of free speech at this time. Note how one of Hutchinson's supporters cites a Bible verse, Proverbs 25:9, to criticize the ministers. That would carry some weight in a roomful of puritans. A careful reading of the trial record gives good arguments both for and against Hutchinson. Hutchinson wanted the ministers to testify under oath because she felt that they understated the amount of pressure they put on her to talk. There was some sympathy for her demand that the ministers testify under oath; convictions at this time normally required a confession or two sworn witnesses, and the bible endorsed oaths as a way of ending controversies.

A defense that Hutchinson only started to raise at her trial was that she was right and the ministers wrong. This would be the strongest defense of all, if it could be sustained.

Revelations were a borderline phenomenon in puritanism, not something that ministers encouraged, but not something that they always completely rejected, especially if they came in the form of Scripture verses. Hutchinson's revelations took the restrained form of scripture verses coming to mind. Given her impressive piety, she probably would have gotten by with nothing more than an occasional informal rebuke for them, had they not formed the basis for her attacks on the ministers. Pay attention to Winthrop's careful explanation of why he regarded Hutchinson's as unacceptable.

Cotton was the only person to defend her Scripture revelation about the destruction of the Court. Those revelations, he claimed, contained no new religious doctrines; therefore, they did not make her a heretic. She did not assert that she would be delivered by a miracle, so she was not blasphemously presumptuous (Hutchinson probably expected to be rescued by the return of Henry Vane). Thus, while he could not endorse Hutchinson's claim, neither could he condemn it. He had no proof, after all, that God would not destroy the General Court.

As Cotton's purely religious defense of Hutchinson indicates, she was being tried in not just any English Court. This was a court of puritans trying a fellow puritan. That meant that their concerns were not always legal ones, in the narrow sense of that term. Many of them had defied English laws when they regarded those laws as breaking the word of God. For Hutchinson's words to be crimes in puritan eyes, they not only had to be illegal, but against the Bible. The synod of churches that had met in September had concluded that the ministers did not preach a covenant of works. But in Massachusetts, synods had no way of enforcing their verdicts. John Wheelwright, at his sentencing hearing a few days before Hutchinson's trial, tried to argue the theological issues between him and the other ministers over again. Hutchinson raised them again when she mentioned her English scriptural revelations, but those revelations were immediately overshadowed by her revelation about the destruction of the Court. Had she tried and succeeded in convincing a majority on the Court that the ministers did preach a covenant of works, she would not have been convicted.

Strategies for Thinking Like a Puritan

To make your arguments—either for or against Mrs. Hutchinson—you must understand the mindset of seventeenth-century puritans in Massachusetts. The sections that follow outline the basic ideas.

The colonists who founded Massachusetts were poised between the Middle Ages and the modern world, and in many ways, they helped to bring the modern world into being. Their passionate struggles over how far they could tolerate a diversity of religious opinions in a colony committed to religious unity were part of a larger historical process that led to religious freedom and the modern concept of separation of church and state. Their deep concern over the dangers arbitrary government and Roman Catholicism presented to the people's liberties and to the Protestant societies being created in the New World would pass down to the American Revolution and beyond.

Institutions of Massachusetts Puritanism

THE TRUTH OF THE BIBLE AND ERROR

Puritans passionately held that the Bible had a single truth and that all Christians should follow that truth. They were a very diverse movement, but they wanted a community built around unity of belief and worship. They believed that God wanted the same and would be angry if the government and churches of Massachusetts failed to provide it. They fled England not because it did not allow religious freedom, but because it was not following God's will.

Thus, handling disagreements gracefully was not something that came easily to puritans. Were your opponent's ideas not supported by the Bible? If you decided they were not, then how dangerous were they? Religious errors were not all alike. Some were mild and could be tolerated, if necessary, for the sake of Christian unity. A dangerous error, though, was one that could lead to heresy. A heresy was an error that would lead to hell. Puritans would agree that any error that kept you from relying properly on Jesus for salvation was at least very dangerous, but they would not necessarily agree about which errors fell into that category. There was no official puritan creed, and while there was a broad consensus about many religious issues, there was no complete agreement about what constituted errors in the first place.

Given that puritans saw the world in a vast struggle between the forces of God and the forces of the Devil (whose chief earthly agents were Antichrist and the Catholic Church), it was tempting to see sinister forces at work behind the people with whom you disagreed.

Quarrels between puritans in England were usually buried beneath the larger struggle with opponents like Archbishop Laud. But in Massachusetts, puritans were in control of religion and had the means of enforcing uniformity of belief. The colony undoubtedly had many religious quarrels that left no trace in the very scanty documentation that has survived from its early years. But we do know of a few before the explosive disputes around Anne Hutchinson broke out, with the case of Roger Williams being the most prominent.

THE MASSACHUSETTS GOVERNMENT

The Massachusetts government consisted of a General Court with a Governor, Deputy Governor, Assistants, and Deputies. The deputies represented towns and were elected by the adult male church members (freemen) in those towns. The rest were elected by all the freemen in the colony. Voters had to be adult male church members, and elections were yearly.

THE GENERAL COURT AS A LEGAL COURT

The General Court, besides being Massachusetts' legislature, was the most important law court in the colony. It decided cases by majority vote and its members functioned as judges, jury, prosecutors, and to a lesser extent, defense advocates. As in English courts, defendants were considered innocent until proven guilty. However, they had few legal rights. They did not know the evidence against them in advance, and they were not allowed legal counsel during trials. Their witnesses could not be sworn. Judges were not expected to maintain strict impartiality, and standards of proof were far less rigorous than they are today.

MASSACHUSETTS CHURCHES

Massachusetts churches normally had two ministers. One of these, the teacher, was in charge of doctrine, while the other, the pastor, handled the practical and moral guidance of the congregation. The pastor had one or two laymen, ruling lay elders, to help him. The men of the congregation elected all these officials. If a church member was suspected of grievous moral failings or heretical opinions, the church would give him or her a trial. If the males in the congregation found the member guilty, he or she would either be admonished or excommunicated. The churches could hold meetings of all the churches (synods) to debate and issue formal statements on theology and church governance. While the conclusions of those meetings were considered authoritative, the churches had no way to compel individual churches to follow them. The churches considered themselves to be part of the Church of England, although their practices were almost uniformly in violation of the laws of that church. Even many English presbyterian puritans thought that the Massachusetts puritan churches were dangerously democratic.

CHURCH-STATE RELATIONSHIP

The Massachusetts puritans wished to create a unified Christian society. The concept of religious freedom was alien to them. Yet at the same time, following the teachings of the great Protestant John Calvin (1509-1564), they believed in a strict separation of church and state. Church elders could not serve as public officials, and vice versa; the churches could excommunicate members, but they could not give secular punishments like fines and imprisonment. The state—the General Court—ordered residents of Massachusetts to attend church and to financially support the ministers, but beyond that it was not supposed to interfere with the churches. This relationship between church and state worked on the assumption that everyone agreed about what true religion was (and remember that you had to be a church member to vote or run for office).

PURITANISM AND WOMEN

Massachusetts, like England, was a patriarchy: Men ruled. Women were an inferior sex, and married women like Hutchinson had few legal rights. When possible, they were expected to focus on the arduous tasks of being wives, mothers, and household managers. The Bible commanded them to submit to their husbands. Puritan preachers reiterated that command, while complaining how frequently wives ignored it.

However, the situation for puritan women was not as one-sided as it sounds. Ministers also warned husbands that all positions of power tended to degenerate into tyranny. Their wives were their companions whom it was their duty to love, not their slaves, and they told wives that they need not quietly submit to beatings or adultery. It was a Christian wife's duty to lovingly criticize her husband about his failings and a husband's duty to accept such criticisms. Ministers warned women that they were not to love and obey their husbands more than they loved and obeyed Christ. If they had to choose, they were to choose Christ.

Women took this duty to obey Christ above earthly authorities seriously. Defiant puritan women appeared in large numbers in the church courts and even in prison. On a more positive note, they could acquire a great deal of prestige as spiritual counselors, as Hutchinson did. In other words, Hutchinson would never have been accused of overstepping her place as a woman because of her popularity, had she not disagreed with the ministers. Moreover, she was punished no more severely than the most vociferous men. However, there is also no question that the authorities had an extra edge of irritation in dealing with Hutchinson that they did not have with the men precisely because she was a woman stepping out of her place. Note the dispute between Winthrop and Hutchinson in the trial record as to whether or not she stepped out of her proper role as a woman. Hutchinson insisted that she did nothing inappropriate.

LIBERTY

A liberty was a privilege or right granted a person or organization. Many, but not all, English males had the liberty of voting for members of Parliament, while all English people had the liberty of trial by jury. You might have the liberty to fish in a certain river or sell your goods in a certain market, etc. Liberties were protected by the rule of law. Rulers who did not bind themselves to laws or who bent the laws to their own purposes were arbitrary rulers and well on their way to becoming tyrants.

The greatest liberty of all was Christian liberty. This liberty was the ultimate privilege of being able to become a true follower of Christ.

In puritan eyes, civil and Christian liberty were bound together. The Pope, under the spirit of Antichrist, was the ultimate tyrant, answerable to no earthly laws, violating the laws of God, and persecuting true Christians. The Spanish monarchy, the Pope's greatest ally and England's greatest enemy, spearheaded a relentless Catholic effort to overturn Protestantism, and English Protestants looked upon that monarchy as tyrannical.

The Massachusetts puritans found it no coincidence that King Charles treated English Catholics gently even as he began to ignore English laws in order to raise money or that Laud was not harshly anti-Catholic and cracked down on puritanism. Tyrannical government and sympathy with Catholicism, puritans thought, went hand in hand. In Massachusetts, both in church and state, puritans put a great deal of effort into seeing that rulers could be controlled by those whom they ruled so that they could not engage in arbitrary rule.

Hutchinson's allies saw their opponents as violating both the laws of Christ and their liberties as English people, and for them, this combination was completely predictable (see Henry Vane and John Winthrop's debate about the Immigration order, included in the Primary Documents section of the Appendix). Hutchinson's opponents saw her brand of liberty as little more than anarchy (see John Winthrop's discussion of liberty, included in the Primary Documents section of the Appendix).

THE THEOLOGY OF PURITANISM

Few modern readers can gain ready admittance to the seventeenth-century puritan mind. The religious views are at odds with many modern notions and concepts. The puritans' belief in original sin contravenes the common assumption of the innocence of children and the worth of the individual and the puritan notion that God had predestined most people to eternal suffering violates contemporary sentiment in favor of a kindly God—or of none at all. Moreover, the puritans presumed that their listeners and readers were intimately familiar with the Bible. They hammered home points merely by alluding to the pertinent Biblical citation. Finally, the points of doctrine were so hotly disputed and fraught with such awesome implications that puritan ministers expressed themselves in complex analyses that drew on the convoluted language and methods of the scholastic theologians of the Middle Ages and whose meaning is often inaccessible to us.
For these reasons and others, we are often inclined to skirt the strange intellectual world of seventeenth-century puritans or interpret it in familiar terms: as a source of secular rituals of family and community, such as Charlie Brown's Thanksgiving or, conversely, as an embodiment of sexual and political repression, such as Nathaniel Hawthorne's *The Scarlet Letter*, an indictment of puritan hypocrisy, or Arthur Miller's *The Crucible,* a repudiation of repression by religious authorities.

But these renderings of the puritan minds would have been unrecognizable to the puritans themselves. Such views neglect the appeal and power of these beliefs three and a half centuries ago, as doctrinal disputes erupted into bloody civil wars and wars of conquest. The modern world emerged out of the ravages of this turbulent time; we cannot understand its origins, nor those of the United States, without making an effort at apprehending what these disputes—these tangled thickets of obscure words—were all about.

The central issue debated by Hutchinson and her opponents was how believers could know that they had been saved and were going to go to heaven. To understand what was at stake with that issue, it is necessary to understand the sweeping context in which puritans placed it. If the following is alien to your beliefs, treat it as a mythic story of cosmic dimensions involving extraordinary supernatural beings and yet a story in which every single individual human being has a critical involvement.

Before time began, God (a Trinity, the Father, Son, and Holy Spirit, but at the same time one God) decided to create human beings. The puritans, following the great Protestant John Calvin, believed that God **predestined** most of these still-uncreated humans to go to hell as a demonstration of His justice. A very few, the **elect**, would go to heaven as a demonstration of His mercy.

In order to enact this plot, God created the world. He made a **covenant of works** with the first man, Adam. Under this covenant, or agreement, as long as Adam (and Eve) continued to perfectly obey God's will, God promised that they and all their posterity would continue in perfect happiness. But Adam and Eve, tempted by the devil, ate the fruit that God had forbidden to them. They thereby broke the covenant of works, as God had predestined would happen, in order to insure that His story line would be executed.

When Adam and Eve ate the forbidden fruit, their original holiness was destroyed by their sin. Just as everyone would have gone automatically to heaven if Adam had stayed holy, now everyone is born with original sin. They are in their nature totally corrupt. No matter what good they might do, their hearts are full of evil and selfishness that can break out at any time. They deserve to go to hell because of their wickedness, and that is where all those people God predestined to go to hell end up (damned babies got the easiest room in hell, proclaimed a popular Massachusetts poem).

Although the covenant of works is still in effect, no one can fulfill its terms and be perfectly holy, because everyone sins. People who try to be saved to the slightest degree by their own piety or deeds are going to hell.

For those fortunate few people God predestined for salvation, He made a **covenant of grace**. Jesus on the cross took the guilt and punishment that their sin deserves and so they are spared hell, not because of anything that they do, but because of Christ's sacrifice and God's mercy. The elect are saved by God's free grace and His measureless love for them, not by their works.

When the total number of the predestined elect have been born and saved, Christ will return for the Last Judgment. The world and time will come to an end, while heaven and hell will endure for eternity as monuments to God's glory, mercy, and justice. It was generally believed in the seventeenth century that the end of the world would soon happen.

How does this story intersect with the earthly lives of ordinary people, according to puritans? These people go about their lives paying little attention to the cosmic drama in which they are embedded. Perhaps they are lukewarm Christians, leading a more-or-less good life, complacent and convinced that Christ is their savior. But at some point, perhaps through the preaching of a fiery puritan preacher, they might realize that they have not really scrutinized themselves and not really faced a deeply buried smugness, a sense that they are fundamentally sound. They are still under a covenant of works, still convinced deep down, even unconsciously, that they will go to heaven because they deserve to. And that is a sure sign, they realize with horror, that they are in a covenant of works and are going to hell.

At this point, panic and terror set in. The once complacent Christian starts to discover the extraordinary hollowness of her good behavior and the endless depths of her sinful nature. The more she discovers, the further away from God she feels. Terror and even a suicidal despair set in. If the person in whom this is happening is in the covenant of grace and predestined to be saved, then this process is all to the good. Only the gut-wrenching personal discovery of how incapable humans are to save themselves prepares them to truly depend on Christ for salvation.

The very moment in this agonizing process that genuine, total dependence on Christ occurs is the moment of conversion, and in that twinkling of an eye, a number of complex supernatural events take place. The convert receives true **faith** that Christ died for him or her. As part of the same event, God **justifies** the individual. **Justification** is a divine edict that because of Christ's sacrifice, God absolves the convert of the guilt of her sins. She is in His eyes, from henceforth, just, and she may go to heaven. God then begins changing her corrupt human nature by making it holy again, in a process called **sanctification**. That process is partial; no human can become perfectly holy in this lifetime.

Predestination might seem totally arbitrary and grossly unfair. Puritans, however, insisted that it was a profoundly comforting doctrine. Once your membership in the covenant of grace had been confirmed by justification, you could have **assurance of salvation**. If God had predestined you to heaven, then, regardless of whether you sinned again, you would get there. God would not change His mind. Assurance was the safe harbor after the emotional storms of conversion, and, puritans claimed, it brought with it the most profound peace and joy that life could give.

But how was an ordinary puritan supposed to read God's mind? The stakes were dizzily high: heaven, if you found assurance; hell, perhaps, if you did not, and you knew that most people went to hell.

Two Paths to Assurance of Salvation

The following sections contrast the path as outlined by Winthrop and the orthodox ministers and that of Mrs. Hutchinson.

FOR THE PERSON WHO FOLLOWS WINTHROP AND THE ORTHODOX MINISTERS

The turmoil of preparation leads you to a changed life. You eagerly attend sermons. Rather than getting drowsy as before during the two hours or more of their duration, you hang on the minister's every word. You spend much time with other puritans, discussing the Bible and your spiritual lives. You pray a great deal when you are alone and vigilantly watch your thoughts for sinful impulses. You feel utterly devoted to Christ. If, before salvation, your eye wandered toward the handsome frame of your neighbor, you resist that temptation more successfully. If, before, you took great pride in your cooking or work with a scythe, now you find it easier to exhibit true Christian humility. If, before, you lost your temper or responded in kind when a neighbor spoke ill of you, now you find yourself at peace and you forgive those who harm you. You clearly are not the same person you were before justification, before God's gift of grace. [This first paragraph is the same as in the Hutchinsonian view; what follows is not.]

You long to know that the great event of justification has indeed occurred. But the ministers tell you that the event itself is God's secret. You cannot know directly of God's decisions and actions. You take comfort from the fact that ministers have many times preached that changes like the ones you have been experiencing could indicate that God has justified and saved you. They tell you that the Bible is a set of precepts and divine rules. They say that it contains promises from God that certain behavior is proof of salvation. They have drawn up checklists from those promises.

Do you thirst after the gospel more than food?

Do you long to hear sermons?

Do you scrutinize your heart for the first sign of sin?

Do you mourn your sin whenever it emerges?

Do you regard that struggle with sin as a constant battle?

Do you put all of your trust in God?

And, as the ministers reiterate again and again, do you love your fellow puritan saints, with whom you are destined to spend eternity praising God in heaven? That love is a sure sign that you are saved.

When you seem to measure up well to that list, you take comfort and assurance. At night you sleep more soundly and by day you walk with a lighter step and a fuller heart. You feel contented. This means that God has sanctified you, and this can only happen after He has justified you—selected you as among those who will dwell with him forever in heaven. You are not proud of your better behavior and godlier thoughts, because you know that this new holiness comes from God. You are grateful to God for extending to you His gift of grace. You feel assured of salvation.

But you are still a mortal being and sometimes you sin. When you see your neighbor bathing in a stream, perhaps you think troubling thoughts. Or perhaps you thrill with satisfaction at cooking a delicious pie or clearing a field of a huge boulder, or you explode in anger when a neighbor steals some of your chickens and builds a stone fence that encloses some of your land. You compare this behavior with the minister's list of evidences of sanctification: You realize that you have not measured up as well as in the past. And now you have doubts about whether you have been truly saved. You pray for repentance and throw yourself with renewed zeal into a life of holiness. You study the list, repeatedly. You study your behavior and thoughts. You continuously interrogate yourself to make sure that you are showing signs of holiness. In your anxiety about your salvation, you can become desperate, even suicidal.

And yet, if you are truly justified, eventually you find signs of your God-given holiness again. You again feel confident—assured—of your salvation. You thank God.

But perhaps yet again you lapse into sin, and once more you worry that your hopes of salvation were mere delusions. You recall that the ministers assure you that this doubt is a good thing. It is making you a stronger and better Christian. Again you try hard and ruthlessly scrutinize yourself. You find assurance again, until the next time that you stumble. After many years of this cycle of assurance, doubt, and then renewed assurance, a steadiness emerges in your faith. You know that you will come out of your doubts and that you will always again find your feet in firm footing in godliness.

This confidence—assurance—has become steadier and stronger than at the outset. You find it easier now to weather your periods of doubt, and they are less frequent. You know that you are fortunate. The ministers caution that some never find this assurance. You also know people who impress you with their holiness, but they say that they never achieve this confidence, or they do not achieve it with your consistency.

You know some persons—many of them are pious and well-meaning—who gather at Anne Hutchinson's house and at the homes of others who adhere to similar views. Such persons scorn your beliefs. They say that your fervent self-examination is mere self-deception. They say that you are destined to suffer eternal torments in hell. They say that those who are truly saved know it in their hearts, having received some sort of revelation from God. Indeed, they cast doubt on your Christian humility: How dare you claim that your puny attentiveness to the teachings of the orthodox ministers, or that your zealous resolution to adhere to God's laws and those of the General Court, can be proof that the great God loves you? All that matters, they say, is God's gift of grace. They have it, and those who believe as you believe and feel as you feel do not. And yet their proof of their grace—a proof that feeds their arrogant assurance—is nothing more, perhaps, than a passage of Scripture that they happen upon when they spill a plate of peas onto the Bible—the word of God speaking to them!

You know that God chose His Saints for a reason. The Bible says as much. The **Elect** will doubtless have important work to do when they sit at the right hand of the Lord in heaven. He wants humility of His saints, not arrogance; He wants them to subject their thoughts and actions to relentless self-examination and self-criticism, not to passively await His grace. Hutchinson's followers demean God and His works by saying that nothing much is expected of them. And in this state of indolent self-satisfaction, they lead themselves to flout God's laws, demean His ministers, and place themselves above His word. You cannot allow this.

FOR THE ADHERENT OF ANNE HUTCHINSON'S VIEWS

The turmoil of preparation leads you to a changed life. You eagerly attend sermons. Rather than getting drowsy as before during the two hours or more of their duration, you hang on the minister's every word. You spend much time with other puritans, discussing the Bible and your spiritual lives. You pray a great deal when you are alone and vigilantly watch your thoughts for sinful impulses. You feel utterly devoted to Christ. If, before salvation, your eye wandered toward the handsome frame of your neighbor, you resist that temptation more successfully. If, before, you took great pride in your cooking or work with a scythe, now you find it easier to exhibit true Christian humility. If, before, you lost your temper or responded in kind when a neighbor spoke ill of you, now you find yourself at peace and you forgive those who harm you. You clearly are not the same person you were before justification, before God's gift of grace. [This first paragraph is the same as in the orthodox view; what follows is not.]

But you do not draw any conclusions from the changes in the way you think or behave. You might still be in a covenant of works, acting holy out of your own effort to prove that you are good. Perhaps you are trying to prove your goodness—even your godliness—to others; or perhaps you force yourself to do good deeds and think good thoughts in an effort to persuade yourself that you ARE of God. But you know that your thoughts and actions do not influence God's thoughts and actions. It would be a blasphemous presumption to imagine that your inconsequential thoughts and actions can tell you about the will of God.

For you, the Bible is a set of rules and precepts, but it can be more than that. Its words can suddenly be filled with divine life, and God can communicate to you directly through them. You believe that such a communication takes place at justification, the moment where God imparts His gift of grace to you. At that time, God sends a signal to you that He has saved you. You might be so mired in sin and self-doubt as to miss the first message, but God will continue to repeat it.

One day, perhaps when you are at prayer, you receive such a direct sign. A verse like "Thy sins have been forgiven" rises up in your mind with exceptional force and immediacy. A feeling of peace and contentment spreads through your body and warms your soul. You realize that God is telling you that you have been saved. This may be the actual moment of justification, or it might be a later and stronger confirmation of an earlier signal, one that you perhaps failed to notice. Either way, now you know that you are saved. Often your whole person is infused with an ineffable joy.

You continue to behave piously: You do not act in such a godly manner in a spirit of self-interrogation, always seeking an answer to the question of whether you are truly saved. Rather, you think godly thoughts and you behave in a godly fashion out of gratitude and love for the God who has saved you. The Bible is no longer a set of rules; rather, it is a set of suggestions on how to express your love for God. Your new holiness —sanctification—confirms that you are saved, but it does not form the basis of your assurance. The basis of your assurance came when God sent His signal.

Yet you know that no one is perfect. You are still a mortal being, and you may succumb to temptation. When you do, you are shaken; and you grieve that you have sinned against the God who has been so good to you: the God who has given you eternal life and made you one of His saints. But you do not question your salvation, because your salvation does not depend on your deeds or thoughts. You do not seek proof in your behavior of your justification, because your behavior, disconnected from God, offers no such proof. Nor is there any benefit to doubting. It does not make you a better Christian; it only keeps you away from God.

Rather, you focus on the power and love of Christ until you again receive a direct sign from God. Perhaps another scripture verse will reveal itself to you that tells you of your salvation. Those verses will grow ever stronger in their impact, and they will bring unspeakable joy. Eventually God through Scripture verses may tell you what is happening and will happen in the world around you.

Your assurance is a priceless gift; you cherish it. You are saddened that not all people have received such a gift. But when poor unfortunates present themselves for admission to puritan churches and they cite their doubts and anxieties and ceaseless self-searchings as PROOF that they have been justified, you are alarmed. You know that they have not only deluded themselves, but they have also demeaned the NATURE of God's gift of grace. They have made it something weak and pale and joyless. And when ordained ministers stand at the pulpit and recite their lists of self-searchings and call on people to examine their actions for evidence of God's grace, you know, too, that they are not saved; and you know that their preaching not only deceives everyone else but also cheapens the glory that is God's gift of grace. This is akin to what the Catholic Church in Rome has done for centuries. This you cannot abide and must not abide.

PRO and CON ARGUMENTS

WINTHROP AND THE ORTHODOX MINISTERS

The ministers had one main positive argument for their insistence that holiness could give assurance of salvation: If we know that sanctification is a result of justification, they argued, why should we not trust it? That is, if justification makes it easier for a person to engage in Christian charity and fellowship, is it unreasonable to assume that a person who does good works for the poor and is the best of Christian neighbors has not been justified? God made clear promises in the Bible that sanctification was a sign of justification. Does God deceive? As long as you can see that your general tendency is to struggle against sin and behave in a holy manner and that you do this not for selfish reasons but for the love of God, you can trust that you have been saved.

The ministers attacked the opinion of Hutchinson's allies for a number of reasons. The most basic was that they saw it as nothing more than an opening for endless self-deception. Wicked people were always looking for a way to convince themselves that they were saved while avoiding the hard work of holiness. The idea that salvation had no requirement of holiness attached to it was called **antinomianism** and went back to the days of the apostles, who fiercely fought it. How convenient to believe that some scripture verse that popped into your head meant that you were saved.

Hutchinson's allies acknowledged that it certainly was a good idea to pay attention to your holiness as a reality check, but, asked the ministers, was this not the same as admitting that you could not trust a scripture revelation that you were saved until you saw yourself transformed? Perhaps Scripture verses could give comfort in the way that Hutchinson's allies described, but they were inevitably subjective. The only reliable evidence of salvation was holiness.

The ministers' concern went far beyond antinomianism, however. Hutchinson and her allies claimed that you could know you were justified when the Holy Spirit darted a verse like 1 Tim. 1:15, "Christ Jesus came into the world to save sinners; of whom I am the chief and principal," into your mind. You would have an overwhelming emotional experience that you were the person being referred to in that verse and therefore that Christ came to save you. But how, demanded the ministers, was it possible that a verse written 2,000 years ago could be about you personally? That was absurd; but more, it was dangerous. If you could make the Bible tell you that you were saved personally, you could make it say anything. No need for the guidance of ministers—whatever Scripture verses that came into your head in whatever sequence they happened to come meant whatever you thought they meant. It was as if you put a powerful automobile into the hands of someone who lacked the training and self-discipline needed to drive safely. The wise and true meaning of the Bible, on which morality and public order depended, would be abandoned, as people acted out whatever they thought their Scripture verses dictated to them. Soon they would take the next step and abandon the Bible altogether, while acting on whatever impulses came to mind.

Protestants had already seen this happen in the bloody rule of the Anabaptists of Münster, Germany. Hutchinson was opening a door for it to happen again in Massachusetts. Now Hutchinson's revelations were prompting her and her supporters to insult the ministers; soon those revelations might tell her supporters to massacre them. It was fear of what might happen in Massachusetts as much as what actually was happening that drove the opponents of Hutchinson and her allies.

We must remember that the debate was made more complicated by the fact that people in Cotton's congregation, including Hutchinson, were quietly playing around with more radical theological ideas, some of which did come from familism.

Hutchinson is good at covering her tracks. Her supporters on the General Court don't believe that the accusations against her are true (they will change their minds in the coming months).

In 1638, the Massachusetts minister Peter Bulkeley commenced a series of sermons that defended the orthodox conception of assurance of salvation. They were subsequently published in London. Here Bulkeley is explaining why sanctification can give assurance of salvation. For Bulkeley, assurance comes through probing and testing yourself. These selections come from *The Gospel Covenant*, 2d ed. (1651), 261, 263. They have been abridged and adapted.

Bulkeley:

Some do deny this way of trial [of assessing ourselves to see if we have been saved], as if no evidence could be had from our sanctification, until we first know our election and justification by immediate revelation of the Spirit [as the allies of Hutchinson insisted]. But if there is no trial and knowledge of our estate to be had by sanctification, then what did Christ mean when he told his disciples, that hereby should all men know them to be his disciples, if they love one another? Joh. 13. What did Paul mean, when he bids us test ourselves whether we be in the faith or no? 2 Cor. 13. David surely was deceived when he said, Hereby I know that I shall not be confounded when I have respect unto all the commandments, if no knowledge of our good estate may be gathered thereby. Yea, to what end did John lay down all those signs and tokens of a blessed estate, which are scattered here and there through the whole first Epistle?

His scope in that epistle being this, even to give to the faithful some certain evidence of their salvation, as is manifest by chap 5. 13. And this being his scope, mark then how frequent and plentiful he is in bringing in evidences of this nature, as now we speak of, as we may see Chap. 1.7. If we walk in the light (of holiness) as he is in the light, then have we fellowship with another (that is God with us, and we with him). So Chap. 2. 3, 4. Hereby we are sure that we know him (so as to have eternal life by the knowledge of him, John 17. 3) if we keep his Commandments; and in verse 29. Know ye that he which doth righteousness is born of him; and in Chap 3. 7, he that does righteousness (walking in the righteousness of a good conscience and upright conversation) is righteous (namely by imputation) even as Christ is righteous; and in verse 9, 10. He that is born of God sinneth not. In this are the children of God known from the children of the Devil, even by righteousness and loving of our brethren. And verse 14. Hereby we know that we are translated from death to life, because we love the brethren. So also verse 18, 19, and 24, and Chap 4. verse 7, 13, 13, 16.

Quest. But some may say, why should we go about to evidence our justification by our sanctification, rather than our sanctification by our justification [as the allies of Hutchinson insisted by arguing that it was only after God had told you that He had justified you that you could trust that your holiness was genuine].

Answ: Our sanctification is more manifest to us than is our justification. It is easier discerned because our sanctification is a work within us, wrought in our own hearts, of which a man cannot but have a sensible feeling in himself.

THE ALLIES OF ANNE HUTCHINSON

The allies of Hutchinson, in responding to the ministers, flipped their main arguments on their head. It was the allies of Hutchinson who were objective and their opponents who were subjective. How could you know that your sanctification was real unless you already knew that God loved you? People in a covenant of works could act impressively holy for a very long time; they could even appear more holy than true Christians. The capacity for people to fool themselves about their motives for their good behavior was endless. The only way to escape the subjectivity of one's own opinions about one's salvation was to be touched by God directly.

Moreover, Christians were supposed to serve God out of love for Him. How could they love Him unless they had already tasted His love? If they were behaving in a pious way because they were hoping to discover by it that they were saved, then they were serving God out of self-interest and fear of damnation, not love. No wonder that they doubted their salvation so often.

Even more seriously, the allies of Hutchinson feared that the ministers' methods were leading people back into a covenant of works. For all practical purposes, they were teaching people to look to themselves, not Christ, for salvation. The implications of that teaching were frightening. At best, the ministers were preventing true Christians from discovering that they had been saved by keeping them looking in the wrong places. At worst, they were undermining the Reformation by keeping the way of finding Christ hidden. In the minds of their opponents, at least, the orthodox ministers' teaching resembled that of the Roman Catholic Church, which emphasized the importance of "works" like the sacraments for salvation. For puritans, Roman Catholicism was as much a state of mind as it was the actual church. You could easily suspect your opponents of being infected by the "spirit of popery." The Catholic Church also persecuted Protestants, just as the opponents of Cotton and Hutchinson were doing. Behind the Catholic Church was Antichrist himself.

THE MINISTERS' OWN WORDS (IN SUPPORT OF HUTCHINSON)

Hutchinson left very few words behind her. But the ministers John Cotton and John Wheelwright were for a long time her allies, and she would have agreed with their arguments below. Both ministers are explaining that just as we are saved through Christ, we can only know that we are saved through direct knowledge of Christ, not indirectly through sanctification. The first example is from John Wheelwright's 1637 fast day sermon, which has been printed in Charles H. Bell, ed., *John Wheelwrigh,t* Prince Society Publications 9 (1872) and David D. Hall, *The Antinomian Controversy, 1636-1638* (1968, rev. ed., 1990). The second is from John Cotton, *A Treatise of the Covenant of Grace* (1659), 150-1. Both have been abridged and adapted.

> ### Wheelwright:
>
> Truly, both in point of justification, and the knowledge of our justification by faith [knowledge of justification is the same as assurance of salvation], there must be nothing in the world revealed but Christ Jesus. No other doctrine under heaven is able to justify any, but only the revelation of the Lord Jesus Christ. I

am not ashamed of the Gospel, says Paul, for it is the power of God to salvation, 1 Romans 16. How? For in it, the righteousness of God is revealed [Romans 1, 17].

Therefore when the Lord is pleased to convert any soul to Him, He does not reveal to him some work [of holiness within him], and from that work carries him to Christ. But there is nothing revealed but Christ. If men think to be saved because they discover some work of sanctification in them, as hungering and thirsting [for Christ] and the like, if they are saved, they are saved without the Gospel. No, no, this is a covenant of works, for in the covenant of grace, Christ is our righteousness [i.e., we are saved by Christ's righteousness], and so [in the same manner] for the knowledge of our justification by faith, nothing is revealed to the soul but only Christ and His righteousness freely given.

If men have revealed to them some work of righteousness in themselves, such as love to the brethren and the like, and hereupon they come to be assured that they are saved, this is not the assurance of faith, for faith has Christ revealed for its object.

Cotton:

Do not lead a man [who is worried about his salvation] to see his faith or any other qualification, therein to satisfy himself [that he is saved]. But if I would help and comfort such a soul, I would declare to him what the Lord has done for us in Christ. I would show him all the treasures of the rich grace of Christ, how he loves freely without any merits in us. I would tell him how freely the Lord Jesus Christ does invite men to come to him, that have neither money, nor money's worth. And if the Lord take delight to do him good by my mouth, he will convey his Spirit of grace in some such word as I have spoken unto him."

The key Bible verse for Cotton and Wheelwright to support their argument about assurance was Romans 8:1: "The Spirit itself beareth witness with our spirit, that we are the children of God." For them, and Hutchinson, this verse meant that assurance had to come at first as a message from the Holy Spirit. They read a similar meaning in 1 John 3: 24: "Hereby we know that he abideth in us by the Spirit which he has given us." Similarly, Ephesians 1: 13-14 said that "after that ye believed, ye were sealed with that holy Spirit of promise, which is the earnest [guarantee] of our inheritance," and a few verses later (17), the apostle Paul told the Ephesians that he was praying that God "may give you the spirit of wisdom and revelation." Any Bible verses speaking of other methods of finding assurance had to be referring to secondary methods. Otherwise, the Bible was giving contradictory messages.

To Cotton and Wheelwright, the Bible also strongly suggested that the doubt and anxieties of many puritans were incompatible with a state of salvation. Romans 8:15 promised that "ye have not received the spirit of bondage again to fear: but ye have received the Spirit of adoption, whereby we cry, 'Abba Father.'" Romans 7: 6 said that "we should serve in newness of spirit, and not in the oldness of the letter [of the law]." Similarly 1 Peter 1:8 told believers that "ye rejoice with joy unspeakable and full of glory," while Hebrews 8:11 promised that "they all shall know me [God], from the least to the greatest." Acts 3:53 told of how "the disciples were filled with joy, and with the Holy Ghost."

More Sources and a Warning

The above is only the tip of the iceberg concerning the debates in this controversy. A reader plunging into the original sources will quickly discover that the question of whether you found assurance from sanctification or from revelations led to a host of further questions. What was the precise order of the process of justification? How did the souls of believers become united to Christ? How did sanctification work? The more the puritans of Massachusetts argued, the more they found to argue about.

Extended debates between the ministers and Cotton can be found in Hall, *Antinomian Controversy*. They are not easy to for a student to negotiate, since they are conducted in highly technical language and often pursue a variety of complex related issues raised by the fundamental debate. You can find a fairly accessible defense of the orthodox position on assurance and sanctification on pp 72-75, (from "fourth prop." through "sixth prop."). Cotton's response runs from pp. 120-142, but it is stiffer going. Cotton gives a more accessible explanation of his position from pp. 177-192 ("The Second Question").

ANOTHER PERSPECTIVE

As one reads through the arguments between Hutchinson and her allies and their opponents, the dispute sometimes seems to be a clash between two personality types. Hutchinson's side was mystical and poetical, the other practical and logical, and neither side was prepared to concede the validity of the other's approach to the divine. Hutchinson's allies took it for granted that their spiritual encounters were true. Asking for more evidence was, as they put it, like holding a candle to the sun. On the other hand, if you did not experience Scripture verses with the intensity that Hutchinson did, you had to be deeply suspicious of the heavy value they put on that experience. Holiness was tangible, measurable, a gift from God and a blessing to society, while revelations were probably nothing more than a mixture of hot air and emotionality, if, more ominously, they were not sent by Satan to damn you and destroy Massachusetts' Christian society. If they gave you comfort, fine, but to claim that they were a reliable way to read God's mind was nonsense.

Terms to Memorize

ANTICHRIST:

Next to Satan, the greatest adversary of Christ, but will masquerade as Christ's most fervent supporter. Puritans assumed that the Pope was Antichrist, but they believed that Antichrist's influence pervaded the Church of England.

ANTINOMIANISM:

The belief that those whom God has saved are freed from the commanding power of His laws. They obey God purely out of love, not out of duty or fear of punishment if they do not obey Him. Most puritans considered antinomianism simply as an excuse for ceasing to struggle against sin.

COVENANT OF GRACE:

The agreement God made for the salvation of the elect. Jesus on the cross took the guilt and punishment that the sins of the elect deserve. Because of Christ's sacrifice, the elect go to heaven.

COVENANT OF WORKS:

An agreement made between God and the first man, Adam. As long as Adam (and Eve) continued to perfectly obey God's will, God promised that they and all their posterity would continue in perfect happiness. The covenant of works is still in effect, but no one can fulfill its terms because everyone is born with original sin from Adam and Eve's disobedience to God. If you accuse someone of "going in a covenant of works," you are claiming that they still believe, consciously or unconsciously, that the covenant of works is still an available means of salvation, making it possible for an individual to achieve salvation through righteous action (adhering to the laws of God). It is highly insulting. To call someone "legal" is the same thing (they think they can be saved by following God's laws).

THE ELECT:

Those humans and angels whom God predestined to go to heaven.

FAITH:

The acceptance of Christ as one's savior. Faith, if genuine, puritans insisted, is purely a gift of God, given by virtue of the covenant of grace.

FAMILISM:

The Family of Love began in the 16th century in Germany. Familists believed that Christians under the illumination of the Holy Spirit could eventually enjoy perfect union with God and freedom from both sin and the responsibility for it. They believed that their own revelations superseded the Bible. Many of their ideas went back to the murderous, revelation-driven radical Protestant Anabaptists of Münster, Germany, in the 1530s. In England, Familism underwent many, mostly unrecorded, grass-roots mutations.

JUSTIFICATION:

God's pardon of the elect for their original and actual sin and His acceptance of Christ's perfect righteousness in place of their own sinful nature.

PREDESTINATION:

God, before creating the universe, unalterably decreed that some particular men and angels would go to heaven and others would go to hell. As the puritan West Münster Confession of Faith (1646) puts it, "These angels and men, thus predestinated and foreordained, are particularly and unchangeably designed; and their number is so certain and definite that it cannot be either increased or diminished."

SANCTIFICATION:

The creation of a new holiness in believers that follows justification. While people who have not been justified can follow God's laws, puritans called such behavior legal obedience. Whether it was possible to distinguish righteous behavior that came from sanctification (which meant that one had been justified) and righteous behavior that came from legal obedience was one of the hottest areas of dispute between Cotton and the other ministers.

Immigrants and Indeterminates

STRATEGY ADVISORY: PERSUADING THE NEWCOMERS

All immigrants are drawn from a particular sociohistorical context; many—but not all—are substantially "indeterminate" on matters of doctrine. The game will ultimately depend on the vote of the General Court. To win a majority, the best strategy is to persuade the newcomers and other indeterminates—chiefly John Cotton—that your views make the most sense and also that they best accord with the Bible, which most English people of the time regarded as the word of God. The issues are complex. You must plunge into both the details of the historical situation and the nuances of puritan theology. Part of your task is to explain the theological issues to the immigrants, who may be confused. You must read this booklet several times and study it.

This is a closed community, which means that most people know much about each other. But of the immigrants, the community knows relatively little. This is a source of great concern—and curiosity. It is your duty to determine not just if your neighbors are following the laws of God, but also to see into their soul as best you can. Nonetheless, never delude yourself into thinking that you know all about them. You don't, as Calvin would be the first to admit.

For the established people of Massachusetts, most people know who supports Hutchinson and who opposes her. The pro-Hutchinson faction can freely meet and identify themselves, as can the anti-Hutchinson faction (led by Governor Winthrop). Deceit can warrant punishment, either by the Boston congregation or by the General Court. The immigrants can mill around, seeing the sights of Boston; perhaps some will wish to become members of the church.

QUESTIONING IMMIGRANTS WHO SEEK TO BECOME MEMBERS OF THE BOSTON CHURCH

Everyone who seeks to become a member of the Boston Congregational Church must publicly affirm why they believe they have received God's grace (become justified). Examples of actual confessions, and also of questions posed by church members, are included in the "Confessions" Appendix. You will find that those questions may prove useful to you.

Church members may ask whatever they want of prospective members: The congregation has entered into a covenant with God (see Winthrop's speech aboard the *Arbella* in 1630), and they have all promised to ensure that Massachusetts Bay commonwealth keep that promise to follow God's laws as best they can. This begins by ensuring that the community of saints is as pure as mortals can possibly make it.

But what questions should you ask? The answer is, almost anything: because virtually ANYTHING can have theological significance.

Immigrant's age? Younger children, driven by animal impulses and devoid of higher reasoning, are thought to be without God's grace; some parents, of course, perceive evidence in the behavior of infants that suggests early signs of godliness, but few take such "evidence" seriously.

Marital status? God instituted marriage and commanded people to "be fruitful and multiply." When a spouse died, it was expected that the survivor would soon remarry. Unmarried persons were anomalous and slightly inappropriate. For that reason, young single men and women were assigned to live with (and be watched over by) married couples. Even old widows were sometimes regarded as suspect and constituted a disproportionate number of those who, later in the century, were executed for witchcraft. Attitude toward spouse? Accounts by puritans often described their intense love for their spouse and children. Some puritans worried that they had become so infatuated by their sexual attraction to their spouse, or their love of children, that they failed to love God with "all their hearts."

Literacy? Part of the Protestant complaint against the Catholic Church was that the latter relied on the agency of "specialists"—priests, who were often corrupt. The puritans regarded this "intermediary" role as abominable. People should endeavor to understand God's will directly. This required that they read the will of God—the Bible— themselves. Puritan ministers encouraged their congregants to read Scripture for themselves. Back in England, Cotton, like other ministers, had encouraged his congregants to evaluate their ministers' sermons and see whether they were consistent with the Bible. These words returned to haunt him when Mrs. Hutchinson did just that. But for most puritans, it was presumed, the ability to read the Bible was an essential spiritual tool.

Wealth? Conceivably, wealth can be understood as a sign of God's favor, but it can also be a snare to keep one's mind off spiritual goals. Those who have received good fortune in their crops or investments are perhaps under the grace of God, but they will need to be examined carefully. (See, too, Winthrop's theological defense of inequality in his *Arbella* treatise.) People who have been blessed with material abundance are to share it and see that everyone benefits from their blessings. Has the wealth come at the expense of others? Have merchants charged high prices, thereby benefiting from the accidental vagaries of the market to exploit their neighbors? (See, again, Winthrop's injunction that one give to the needy all they need.) Have they helped ministers who were being persecuted for their puritanism or paid for sermons to be preached on market days? Perhaps they helped pay for the publication of puritan books or Bibles. And have they been generous to the deserving poor and to Protestants fleeing from Catholic armies in Europe?

Poverty? Poverty is not automatically a sign of God's disfavor, but the poor have to be virtuous. Did the poverty come from idleness or drinking or excessive indulgence in gambling or whoring? The poor are subject to many temptations, such as stealing and resentment of those whom God has placed in more comfortable situations.

Put more generally: Everyone in the congregation will expect to hear that the applicants went through a time of anguish and intense soul searching. They will all want to know that the applicants now lead sanctified lives. They will all be suspicious, however, if applicants present themselves as too perfect. Everyone expects that people sin.

The trickiest area for the applicants to maneuver through is the issue of what grounds they have to hope that they have been saved. Cotton accepted that a person could be saved before they actually knew it. If an applicant talks about her struggles and about the evidence of holiness within her that gives the individual hope, Hutchinson's allies will not necessarily turn the applicant down as long as she does not insist that she knows absolutely that she is saved and she seems open to further light on the subject. The more applicants talk about their experiences of Christ and his love and the less they talk about their search for evidence of sanctification, the more likely that Hutchinson's allies will approve them. However, the more they do so, the more that Winthrop and his allies will grill them on how closely they pay attention to the evidence of their sanctification.

If the applicant describes a sudden and emotional conversion, the allies of Hutchinson will approve, while Winthrop and his allies will want to make sure that there has been a long-term transformation behind the emotion.

If the applicant expresses no confidence at all that she is saved, both parties might be doubtful as to whether the individual is ready to be a church member. If the applicant expresses strong confidence, Winthrop's party is bound to ask them ask her what happens when she sins. Technically, once you have been assured of salvation, nothing should make you doubt anymore. Cotton says that while sin makes you grievously unhappy that you have broken God's laws, if you have truly had assurance of salvation, it should not make you doubt that assurance, for your assurance should not be based on your sanctification. Winthrop and his allies might accept a confident expression of salvation from an old, experienced puritan, who has had many years to demonstrate faithfulness to God. In a recent convert, they would suspect that it shows a lack of humility and suggests that the convert still does not know how terrible sin is.

Specific questions:

Why did the immigrants leave England?

What do they think about King Charles I and the Church of England under the dreaded Archbishop Laud?

What is their character? Prideful? Humble? Immoral?

Do they know the Bible? Can they recite passages from memory?

Why do they think that they are saved? Do they ever doubt?

But remember: Perhaps God gave His most precious gift of grace to the most miserable worm on earth. Though His justice and mercy are perfect, His ways are inscrutable. How can mortals ever know for sure?

Appendix A: Introduction to the Christian Bible

THE BIBLE, PURITANISM, AND YOU

Students in this game must become familiar with the Bible, and yet the Bible is large, complicated, and even contradictory. Some students, especially those who lack interest in the Bible or reject its claims to be the word of God, may wonder why they should be obliged to engage with it. The answer is that whatever one's religious views, the Bible is indisputably a work of tremendous significance. The Bible has long been regarded as a literary masterpiece, and it has figured prominently in the development of many civilizations. Quite apart from its religious significance to Christianity, the Bible is well worth reading and studying, just as one cannot understand America without understanding the puritans. And one cannot understand puritanism without making some sense of the Bible (and for that matter, the language and stories of the Bible were a common currency in America until well into the 20th century).

People in Massachusetts Bay Colony in the 1630s regarded the Bible as the word of God. Opinions on religious matters that could not be sustained by Biblical stories, with specific reference to chapter and verse, were regarded as worthless. As the word of God, the Bible prevailed over all other arguments. "When I am sure that God has said it, I believe it, for in things Divine there can be no sublimer proof than the testimony of God himself," John Cotton declared. The student's task is to find appropriate scriptural references, apply them to various arguments in accord with her assigned views and game objectives, and express them in language that makes sense to others in the class.

Students may chafe at voicing ideas about God that conflict with their personal beliefs or lack thereof. The purpose of "Reacting," however, is to encourage imaginative stretches of this nature. "Reacting" attempts to push students into the minds of people different from ourselves and into their worlds as well. Students thus do not express personal views; rather, they articulate opinions that have been "scripted" for them by their roles.

The "Introduction to the Bible" that follows is to help guide students through the Bible so that they can better understand how seventeenth-century puritans made use of it. Scholars tend to treat the Bible as a collection of historical documents written at different times for different purposes. Puritans, like all Christians at this time, regarded the Bible as a divinely-inspired unity that revealed the will of God. The Old Testament contained the history of God's true church before the coming of Christ, along with prophecies and foreshadowings of that coming. The New Testament was the fulfillment of the Old Testament. The Bible taught the same path of salvation throughout all of its books. Any apparent contradictions between Biblical texts represented the weakness of human understanding, not the flaws of the Bible. Among other things, that conception of the Bible meant that any line from any part of the Bible could be used in support of a theological position.

The Bible consists of writings dating back almost three millennia that record the sacred tradition of Jews and Christians. The Christian Bible is divided into two parts, the Old Testament and the New Testament. The Old Testament is a collection of thirty-nine writings of the ancient Israelites, as well as the Apocrypha, a collection of books that puritans, like most other Protestants, denied was the word of God and did not cite to support religious arguments. The New Testament is made up of twenty-seven books that constitute the foundation of Christianity.

THE GENEVA BIBLE AND THE KING JAMES BIBLE

Puritans in Massachusetts Bay Colony had ready access to **two** versions of the Bible. The Geneva Bible, published in 1560 under the auspices of John Calvin, a leading Protestant thinker, became popular in late sixteenth-century England. It included long commentaries that were sharply critical of Catholicism. In 1604 James I (King of England from 1603-1625), whose relationship to Catholicism was complicated but less hostile, convened a council of scholars to retranslate the Bible from various ancient Hebrew, Greek, and Latin sources. These scholars published the King James Bible in 1611, which was praised then and later for its beautiful prose. It did not include anti-Catholic commentary. The King James Bible was frequently reprinted and became widely accepted amongst English Christians. The King James Bible can be found in searchable online versions at the University of Virginia (http://etext.lib.virginia.edu/kjv.browse.html) and at the University of Michigan (http://www.hti.umich.edu/k/kjv/), among other places. Parts of the Geneva Bible can also be found online, though these sites have not been authenticated, and your college library has been advised to acquire a copy. Both the King James Bible and the Geneva Bible would have been accepted by New England puritans as expressions of the word of God. Scholars have sometimes argued that Hutchinson and her allies preferred the Geneva Bible, but they freely cited both versions.

The Geneva Bible was the first to divide the books into chapter and verse for ready reference. They were written like this: The third verse of the second chapter of Genesis is Gen. 2:3. To indicate a span of chapters or verses, use a hyphen: Gen 2-7:8 or Gen. 3:4-12.

THE OLD TESTAMENT

The First Five Books

The first five books of the Old Testament—Genesis, Exodus, Leviticus, Numbers, and Deuteronomy—were said to have been dictated to Moses directly by God. They are known by Jewish people as the Torah. These books tell the story from the creation of the world to the point where the Israelites are about to enter their Promised Land, Canaan; the books emphasize the relationship between God and His people and how those people are expected to behave. Puritans believed that they were the heirs of the Israelites in that they were part of God's true church, just as the Israelites were. Thus, the messages of these books applied to them.

The **Book of Genesis** describes the creation of the world, culminating in the creation of man: "And God said, 'Let us make man in our image, after our likeness,' So God created man in his *own* image." This first man God named Adam and commanded that Adam not eat of "the tree of the knowledge of good and evil," for "in the day that thou eatest thereof thou shalt surely die." According to puritans, this was the institution of the covenant of works, since its implicit promise was the exact opposite: Obey me by not eating that fruit, as well as in all other things, and you shall live. From Adam's rib God created the first woman (Eve), but Satan, in the form of a snake, enticed Eve into eating of the forbidden fruit, which she then shared with Adam. God cast Adam and Eve out of the paradise of Eden. He also cursed the snake, promising it that an offspring of Eve would "bruise his heel" (Gen. 3:15). For puritans, this was a prophecy of Christ's birth and a promise of the covenant of grace.

The remaining chapters of Genesis show that human beings persisted in sinfulness. "And God looked upon the earth, and, behold, it was corrupt; for all flesh had corrupted his way." God was disgusted at the spectacle, and in great wrath He decided to destroy mankind with a great flood. But he chose to spare Noah, a just man: "With thee I will establish my covenant." With God's guidance, Noah built a boat that saved him and his family. They were a remnant to repopulate the earth (Gen. 6-9:17). That God would choose some people and destroy others became a central tenet of puritan belief: Not all human beings had been "elected" by God for salvation; some (perhaps the great majority, if the kill-ratio of flood is to be a guide) were to be destroyed. Also important for puritans is the point that Noah, though a just man, remained imperfect. Even after the flood, he got drunk and passed out naked in his tent.

The demise of mankind following their expulsion from the Garden of Eden influenced the way puritans thought about the role of government. If left to themselves, human beings in their fallen state would behave in barbarous and sinful ways. They needed governments to restrain themselves and to promote godly behavior. Aboard the *Arbella,* Governor John Winthrop called on the first puritan settlers to "seek out a place to live and associate under a due form of government both civil and ecclesiastical." Religion would be inseparable from the colony's "due form of government." The government, too, would do what God wanted of human beings. Winthrop declared that God had granted the New England puritans a "special commission" which He wanted to be "strictly observed in every article."

The covenant God made with Noah after the Flood (Genesis 9: 8-17) was for puritans another expression of the covenant of grace. The earth repopulated and divided into nations, which became entangled in war. God wanted to raise up a people who would be an example to the rest and who would follow God's commands (Gen. 12:1-3), and he chose the Israelites, promising Abraham, their leader, that He would make them a "mighty nation." Abraham, like Noah, was not perfect—he was at times cruel and fickle—further proof to the puritans that God's grace was not bestowed upon those of impeccable behavior. Puritans (along with St. Paul) took Gen. 15:6—Abraham "believed in the Lord, and He counted it to him for righteousness"—as Abraham's moment of justification. John Cotton argued that Abraham did not need to look to his own holiness to know that God had saved him.

Exodus, the second book, described how the descendants of Abraham had become enslaved in Egypt and how Moses, with the help of God, managed to save them (Ex. 1:8-14, 2-7:18). After a series of miraculous disasters in Egypt

(Ex. 7:19-12:32), the slaves were released and Moses led them out to Mount Sinai. There God made a covenant with Moses's people—the Israelites: they would obey the laws of God and God would protect them and give them a homeland in the Land of Canaan, which they would rename the Land of Israel. God provided the Ten Commandments (Ex. 20) written in stone, and also a vast array of other rules covering everything from what to eat, when to have sex, and how to build a shrine to God. The children of Israel agreed to the Covenant but immediately and repeatedly failed to keep their part of the bargain (see the episode of the Golden Calf, Ex. 32). God always punished the Jews for their failure.

The puritans identified intensely with the Jews of the Old Testament. They were both part of the true church. The Israelites, a people chosen by God, had suffered under the persecution of powerful tyrants and chose to migrate to a new land; there they confronted countless hardships and were wracked with doubts and misgivings. But, with God's help, they prevailed. So, too, the New England puritans, especially the first generation, believed that they were God's saints—his "elect"—who suffered under the persecution of King Charles I and Archbishop Laud. Much as the Israelites made their way across wide seas and inhospitable deserts and experienced plagues and ordeals, the puritans similarly experienced the miserable crossing of the Atlantic and endured countless privations in New England.

Like the Jews, the puritans were in covenant with God, and like the Jews, they could expect God to punish them if they broke that covenant. The notion of a covenant was so central to puritan thinking that Governor John Winthrop, aboard the *Arbella* before it landed on New England shores, gathered the first immigrants and declared:

> We are entered into covenant with Him for this work. We have taken out a commission. The Lord has given us leave to draw our own articles; we have promised to base our actions on these ends, and we have asked Him for favor and blessing. Now if the Lord shall please to hear us, and bring us in peace to the place we desire, then He has ratified this covenant and sealed our commission, and will expect strict performance of the articles contained in it. But if we neglect to observe these articles, which are the ends we have propounded, and—dissembling with our God—shall embrace this present world and prosecute our carnal intentions, the Lord will surely break out in wrath against us and be revenged of such a perjured people, and He will make us know the price of a breach of such a covenant. (A larger section of this speech is included in Appendix B.)

Everyone on that ship understood what a covenant entailed. Hutchinson, her allies, and her opponents all predicted that God would punish Massachusetts if it did not heed them. Much of the remainder of Genesis chronicles the plight of the Israelites.

The remaining books of this section of the Bible, **Numbers, Leviticus, and Deuteronomy**, contain rules and census figures and describe the final arrival of the Israelites at the border of Israel after forty years of wandering in the deserts.

The book of **Joshua** depicts the taking of the Land of Israel through a combination of war and God's mighty acts. The Israelites displaced the local people, killed as many as possible, and destroyed everything in their path at God's order. However, they were not able to completely control the land, and many local people remained; these were subdued more placidly.

The "Historical Books"

The next set of books continues the narrative of the Israelites from their conquest/occupation of Canaan to their return to Jerusalem after the Babylonian Exile. They include **Judges, Ruth, I and II Samuel and I and II Kings**, the "Historical Books." In relating the story of the Israelite kingdoms in Canaan/Israel, the "Historical Books" reflect a bias toward the Davidic line and strict monotheism.

The climax of the nation-building story is the anointing of David as king. He finally managed to defeat the other peoples of the area and establish the largest united Israelite kingdom which included the Sinai. David was also a flawed person. He committed adultery and arranged to kill the husband of his mistress, Batsheva (II Sam. 11). Because of this, the son of his adultery died. However, since Batsheva's husband was dead, David took her as his wife, and she conceived again; this time, she carried the child full term and bore Solomon. David also suffered the indignity of a coup by his favorite son, Absalom, who died during the coup (II Sam. 15:7-18:18, 18:31-19:1). To puritans, David was a striking example of someone whom God clearly predestined for salvation, yet who fell into horrible sins. John Cotton's opponents pointed out that David, even though he was saved, expressed repentance for his sins. Cotton argued in reply that no matter how much David sinned and expressed sorrow for sinning, he never doubted that God had saved him.

Solomon, one of David's sons, became king after him and raised Israel to its greatest extent, both in power and prestige (I Kings 4 and 5 give a sense of the administration and wealth of the empire). Solomon was often referred to as "Solomon the Wise" (see I Kings 5:9-14) and many of the Psalms and Wisdom writings are attributed to him. Most importantly, Solomon built the first Holy Temple in Jerusalem (I Kings 6, 7). After his death a succession crisis split the kingdom, which was never reunited (I Kings 12).

The rest of the history narrative is reported in **Kings, Chronicles, Ezra, Nehemiah, and Esther**. Chronicles is essentially a repeat of Samuel and Kings; both trace the monarchies in Israel and Judah (the two divided kingdoms after Solomon), the various events and wars, etc. of those times. Chronicles and Kings also contain stories about the early prophets (see below). Ezra and Nehemiah were originally a single book and together treat the story of rebuilding the Temple and the Israelite community in Jerusalem after the Babylonian exile (when the Persians conquered Babylonia, they allowed the Israelites to return and rebuild). The final book, Esther, also takes place during the Persian period and is set in a town named Shushan in Persia itself. It is a story about a Jewish princess who saves the Jews of Persia from destruction and shows a woman acting assertively (risking death) to protect her beliefs and her people.

The "Historical Books" are of special importance to New England puritans, who studied these books for examples of how God expected His chosen people to behave and how He punished them when they did not.

The "Wisdom Books"

Following the "Historical Books" are the Wisdom Books, or "Writings," a varied collection that includes discussion of suffering, praise of God, love and desire. These include Job, Psalms, Proverbs, Ecclesiastes, and Song of Solomon (or Song of Songs).

The **Book of Job** is the story of a righteous man who suffers great loss. It addresses issues of human suffering and the nature of God's justice. To puritans, Job showed further that God's will is inscrutable. Job was a nearly perfect man—clearly among the "elect"—and yet God, responding to a challenge from Satan, filled Job's life with misfortune to see if Job would question God's righteousness. But Job's patience endured these trials, and God blessed him in the end with great worldly prosperity.

New England puritans similarly expected that God would test their faith: Those whom God had "elected" to receive eternal life would not necessarily have an easy time of it on earth. The death of a spouse or child, the failure of their crops and the resulting famine, bitter winters that smothered their villages in mountains of snow—these hardships provided a worthy challenge to show the genuineness of their faith. **Job** also might be read to imply that those who lived up to the test, who fulfilled the terms of the contract, might fairly expect—with Job—that their virtue demonstrated that they were among the saved.

Following Job is the **Psalms,** a collection of sacred poems traditionally attributed to King David. Puritans found in the Psalms an endless treasure house of praises of God, advice on how to live, warnings about what happens to the wicked, descriptions of salvation, words of consolation, and foreshadowings of Christ's sacrifice. **Proverbs** and **Ecclesiastes** are both collections of wisdom literature not unlike the sayings of Confucius in some respects. They offer moral advice on many themes, including the value of education and knowledge, the deceptive ways of folly, the futility and frailty of human existence, and the importance of self-discipline in living a godly life. Lastly, the **Song of Solomon** is a beautiful, lyrical, and descriptive love poem. It is erotic and sensual and has been interpreted as a reference to God's love for Israel or, to puritans, of Christ's love for the Church.

Prophetic Books

The final section of the Old Testament consists of the writings of a group of prophets. Prophets existed in Ancient Israel for around 500 years and had three roles: chiding people for moral and religious failings, comforting Israelites and cursing their enemies after exile, and interceding with God on behalf of Israel in attempts to lessen His anger/punishment. There are two kinds of prophets in the Bible: early prophets (i.e. Elijah), who went into ecstasy, dancing, twirling, etc. to bring the word of God; later prophets, who have entire books attributed to them (Isaiah, Jeremiah, etc.) and function as much as constant moral advisors to the people as oracles. Prophecy is cancelled in the book of Zechariah because despite some tests laid out in Deuteronomy, it was becoming too difficult to distinguish the true prophets from the false ones.

Prophets had been the primary source of communicating God's will or word to the people, and prophecy existed in the early Christian church. Around the time prophecy was halted, the Bible was becoming canonized and effectively replaced prophecy as the authoritative vehicle for knowing God's will. A significant issue in the trial of Mrs. Hutchinson occurred when, under sharp questioning from the General Court, she declared that she had received a revelation of her own mistreatment by the magistrates and further believed that God "should deliver me" from "some calamity that will come to me." The orthodox ministers denounced these revelations—these prophecies—and Winthrop declared: "I am persuaded that the revelation that she brings forth is a delusion."

Prophetic books usually contain: a calling from God, commonly a kind of dream or vision; conversations between God and the prophet; and conversations between the prophet and the people, which follow the functions stated above. There are too many prophets to go into detail about each one, but a brief summary of the important points will give you the idea. The destruction and redemption of Jerusalem is a major theme in many of the most important prophetic books, including Isaiah, Jeremiah, Ezekiel, and Lamentations (which is more of an emotional response to the destruction of Jerusalem and the implied rejection of the people by God). These books are also noteworthy for other things: Isaiah warns against moral sins and emphasizes the importance of care for the week and needy (Amos is also particularly emphatic about "social justice"); Jeremiah challenges God and intercedes with Him on the people's behalf; and Ezekiel contains a famous vision of God on a chariot with bizarre sphinx-like angelic beings, which may be the closest description of God in the Bible.

The other prophetic books are known as the "lesser" prophets and tend to be much shorter. There are a few noteworthy ones, however. Daniel is one of the latest books of the Bible (some of the Apocrypha are additions to Daniel) and contains visions and stories that relate to the end of days and the resurrection of dead, designed to offer hope to readers (Jews) oppressed by Antiochus Epiphanes (c. 2nd century BCE). Joel, Hosea, and Micah also portray variations on a "Day of Judgment" or a scene where Israel is put on trial for straying from the commandments. Puritans freely assumed that these books had prophetic descriptions of their own times.

One last notable prophetic book is the **Book of Jonah**. Jonah is a reluctant prophet who tries to escape his calling by fleeing on a ship. God sends a storm that threatens to drown the ship, and Jonah, realizing that it is God's work and that he is endangering the lives of the sailors, volunteers to jump overboard. God sends a giant fish to swallow Jonah and save him, whereupon Jonah realizes that he should probably go on the mission that God asked him to, which was to indict the city of Nineveh for its "evil deeds" and compel them to reform. The book emphasizes that God's mercy is great, regardless of whether people understand it or think it is warranted.

While the puritans treated the history of the Jews as parallel to their own history, they also treated it as parallel to the spiritual history of each believer. Note how the conversion narratives in the Primary Documents section of the appendix use Old Testament verses.

One important part of the message of the prophets was that God was going to send a Messiah, a savior, who would restore the kingdom and power of Israel and restore the people to God's covenant. He would be a new David, who would restore the power and prestige of the nation. The prophet Isaiah, for example, predicted that that God would again destroy the earth and its peoples, though a remnant would remain: like the stump of a fallen tree, from which a new tree would sprout. Mankind's salvation, Isaiah foretold, would come from the birth of a saviour:

> For unto us a child is born, unto us a son is given: and the government shall be upon his shoulder: and his name shall be called Wonderful, Counsellor, The mighty God, The everlasting Father, The Prince of Peace (Isaiah 9:6).

Puritans, like all Christians and the gospels themselves, regarded the birth of Jesus as fulfillment of this and other Old Testament prophecies. Indeed, puritans regarded the Old Testament as prefiguring—anticipating—much of the New Testament. For example, the covenant that God made with Moses (Covenant of Works: to obey the Mosaic law) prefigured the "new dispensation" God provided through the death of Christ, which granted salvation to some people (Covenant of Grace), although how it did so was a matter of intense debate.

In the centuries immediately before Jesus' birth, Israel was in a rebellious and dangerous state. This part of Jewish history is contained in a group of books called the Apocrypha, which the puritans sometimes read but which, in their eyes, carried no more authority than any other ordinary human books. Other Christian groups disagree.

THE NEW TESTAMENT

The New Testament is about the life and death of Jesus, whom puritans, like all Christians, regarded as the savior, or messiah, whose coming they believed had been foretold in the Old Testament.

The "Gospels"

The New Testament begins with four parallel books (**Matthew, Mark, Luke, and John**) which describe the life, death, and resurrection of Jesus. These books are called the "Gospels," which means "good news." They are referred to as "Gospel according to *x,*" not "Gospel of *x,*" implying that each contains the words of Jesus (the "good news") as written down by one of his disciples. Scholars are in profound disagreement about when each of the gospels was written and what their relationship is with each other.

According to the "Gospels," Jesus was a divinely sent teacher who wanted to reform the practices of Judaism and prepare his listeners for the imminent Kingdom of God. Jesus did not write anything himself, and he preached a simple message; his key maxim was to "Love thy neighbour as thyself." He upset many of the powerful leaders among the Israelites by suggesting that the exact observance of the laws in the Torah (which became the first five books of the Christian Bible) and sacrifices at the Temple were not what God really wanted.

Jesus told many stories to make his points. These are called "parables." The parables usually end in a moral for how to behave. Christ's guidance as to a proper life was significant to puritans, who endlessly pondered whether godly behavior was somehow a sign of one's prospects of being among those who would be saved. Thus when John Cotton was being interrogated by the orthodox ministers, who questioned his insistence that holiness could not demonstrate salvation, Cotton cited the parable of the Publican (Luke 18). In the story, the Publican—a Roman tax collector and an admitted sinner—and a Pharisee, a priest who followed the law, went into a temple to pray. The Pharisee thanked God for making him such a holy man while the Publican merely asked God to have mercy on a sinner such as he. And yet, as Luke related: "I tell you, this man [the Publican] went down to his house justified **rather** than the other." This was proof, declared Cotton, that sanctification (adherence to the laws) could not demonstrate justification, and, conversely, that humble sinners, no matter how disreputable, could have been predestined for eternal life.

Jesus was ultimately arrested by the Jewish leaders and executed by the Roman governor. After Jesus' death, his ideas were in the hands of a group of his followers, the twelve apostles. According to the gospels, they had encounters with Jesus, who had risen from the dead. These encounters encouraged them to spread his message and the news of his resurrection. The details of modern Christian theology did not emerge immediately. In fact, it took over 400 years for the major arguments about who Jesus was and what Christianity was all about to take shape.

The Acts of the Apostles

The books that follow the four Gospels include **The Acts of the Apostles,** which describes Christ's ascension into heaven and the first few decades of the Jesus Movement. Acts 2 records the moment when the Holy Spirit descended on the apostles and enabled them to understand who Christ really was. Hutchinson and her allies looked upon the justification of a believer as fundamentally the same transformative experience. Note Acts 2:17: "And it shall come to pass in the last days, saith God, I will pour out of my Spirit upon all flesh: and your sons and daughters shall prophesy, and young men shall see visions and your old men shall dream dreams." Puritans believed that they were in the last days of the world. It is safe to say that Anne Hutchinson gave this verse much thought.

Epistles

Acts is followed by a collection of letters, called "**Epistles,**" most of which purport to be written by Paul, a radical Jewish convert from outside Israel. Paul became the theologian of Christianity and defined most of what became Christian doctrine. His letters also address a variety of practical problems, which arose as the number and diversity of Christians increased. It is important to understand the evolution of the movement as one reads these letters, since they address specific historical church issues (I Corinthians, Titus, Timothy). Many of the obvious contradictions in Paul's letters, such as those regarding women (Titus 2:3-5, Timothy 2:9-14), are no doubt due to the fact that the books attributed to him were in fact written at very different times.

The first major controversy that arose in the early Jesus movement was whether Jesus' teachings were meant for the Israelites alone or for everyone. This was settled in favor of inclusiveness, and Paul began to spread the story of Jesus all around the Mediterranean basin (see Galatians). Another major controversy was whether non-Jewish followers of Jesus needed to follow all of the Jewish dietary practices (Hebrews). This set the stage for a major battle between Paul and James, who may have been Jesus' brother. Paul won this one as well and began the gradual separation of the Israelites from what became known as Christians. For almost a century the two groups often met together in the same synagogues, but gradually animosities broke out and led to many of the anti-Semitic writings found in some of the later letters. These must be viewed as squabbles between the two groups as they worked to go their separate ways.

The final controversy between Paul and James centered on how much one's behavior (works) counted toward salvation and how much of salvation was due only to God's grace. The degree of this controversy is easily seen by comparing Paul's letters to the Romans and the Galatians with the short book of James near the end of the New Testament. Paul is very clear that salvation is done by God's action alone, in spite of our works, while James feels that works are very important to the process. James was a vegetarian who lived an ascetic, celibate life. However, Paul is very clear about a Christian's responsibility to live a proper life (see Galatians 5 for material critical of the Antinomian heresy, and compare Galatians 2:16-21 and 6:8 with James 1:3, 2:24, and 2:26). In fact, Paul's epistles never quite resolve the tension between his insistence that faith alone saves and his demand for pious behavior.

The resolution of the controversy between faith and works may have rested as much in the execution of James in 63 A.D. and the destruction of Jerusalem in 77 A.D. by the Romans as on the intellectual power of the arguments. The destruction of Jerusalem removed much of the Jewish core of the Jesus movement and shifted the power to the Jewish and Gentile Christians dispersed throughout the Roman Empire.

Several crises occurred that also shaped the writings in Paul's letters and the writings attributed to him. The first was that Jesus' early followers were confident that he was going to return as a Messianic figure to expel the Romans and establish God's kingdom on earth. Jesus had indicated that some of his followers would live to see this event. When it did not happen and the original group died off, it was necessary to do some reinventing of the message. The fall of Jerusalem and destruction of the Temple in 77 A.D. was also a very traumatic event for both Christians and Jews. This too can be seen in the letters attributed to Paul.

A second problem was that the earliest church members lived in what would today be called communes. They kept everything in common. They were very egalitarian groups in which gender and social status did not matter. As their numbers grew, this system became unworkable. Thus, Paul's letters often address very basic issues of church organization (Timothy, Titus, I Corinthians). Establishing a unity of belief among the widely dispersed Christian communities was another challenge. Paul's letter to the Colossians is the most striking example of this.

Revelation

The Bible ends with **Revelation**. This visionary book, said to be written by the apostle John on the island of Patmos, was composed as Christians were undergoing persecution. It is filled with strange, violent imagery and predicts the final battle between Christ and His forces and the powers of evil. The puritans assumed that Revelation was about their times and applied its symbolism freely to current events. The allies of Anne Hutchinson who went into exile with her originally planned to call their new colony Patmos but for unknown reasons changed their minds.

For additional examples of puritan interpretation of the Bible, read the "Theology" section of this packet.

ON PREPARING PRAYERS AND SERMONS

Governor Winthrop and his supporters and the Friends of Anne seek to advance "their" theological and political positions. The trial of Anne Hutchinson turns on these theological issues.

You will wish to prepare the theological groundwork in advance of the trial by preaching sermons or challenging the sermons of others. But how? The only essential point to remember is that God, though distant and inscrutable, did seek to communicate with His human creations by transmitting His word through the Bible. All theological suppositions must ultimately be rooted in the Bible, and puritan sermons focused around the Biblical text. A section in this packet provides an introduction to the Bible **as the puritans would have viewed it.** You should read this section before writing any paper to familiarize yourself with the Bible.

If you are feeling lost in the face of a book as huge as the Bible, Web searches for "Bible salvation" or "Bible assurance salvation," and so forth will provide you with an ample supply of specific verses. They may be from more recent translations of the Bible than the puritans used, so check them. Recent translations may be more accurate in some ways than the ones the puritans used, but by definition, these translations do not get you into the mind of the puritans. Also, they are never as good in terms of being works of art. There are many Web sites on the Bible, some of them written by people whose theology resembles that of the puritans, and these too will be of great help.

If you have read the preceding sections of this packet carefully, you should be able to find your way around such Web sites without too much difficulty. There are also many searchable Bibles on the Internet, though they change from year to year. Your instructor may be able to give you a current site. If you're writing a sermon, you can type in key words and find Biblical verses that you can use in your argument. Make sure that you are searching the King James Bible (KJV for short) or Geneva Bible.

If you choose to write a sermon or a response to a sermon, you should be mindful of the following points. Each sermon focused on particular Biblical "**texts**." In theory, the minister's role was to "open" that text, to explain it fully to his congregation. To do this, he elaborated on the verse in a number of ways. First, he read the text. Then, in a section of the sermon called "**doctrines**," he explained the basic meaning of the verse and noted any doctrinal consequences that followed clearly and directly from that meaning. Next came the section called "**reasons**," in which the minister considered the context of the text, compared it with related passages from other parts of the Bible, and discussed the verse in light of principles of nature, common sense, and human experience, according to the rules of reason and logic. Finally, in a section called "**uses**," the minister applied the insights drawn from the preceding sections to the lives of his congregants. The "reasons" and "uses" sections gave the minister opportunities to make what was in theory a simple explanation of the Biblical text apply to issues and situations that faced the community.

Probably few in the class have memorized the entire Bible, or even much of it; few, too, have listened to, much less delivered, long sermons on difficult points of puritan theology. Fortunately, there are resources that make our work easier. You need not sort through the entire Bible; rather, we can simply follow the furrows ploughed by the litigants in 1636 and 1637. Here's how. Your library should include David Hall's *The Antinomian Controversy, 1636-1638* (Duke, 1990), a document collection. That book includes questions that were posed to John Cotton at the outset of the Antinomianism controversy. If you are assigned to Winthrop's faction, then your position has been laid out by Thomas Shepard and by the Church elders; if you are a Friend of Anne's, your position was anticipated, at least in part, by John Cotton. You can follow their reasoning, and their Biblical citations, to determine how you might argue your case.

First, go to Chapter 3: "John Cotton, *Sixteen Questions of Serious and Necessary Consequence,*" in which the Elders of the church pose sixteen questions to John Cotton, seeking to determine if his preaching was antithetical to their own. Recall that Hutchinson came to New England to follow Cotton and claimed to believe only what he taught and no more. Was *he* in fact the source of all the problems? Or had Hutchinson modified his ideas and made them more radical? Did Cotton change his mind in the course of the controversy? Do his later writings coincide with his earlier ones?

You should regard these letters almost as if they were a foreign language that needs to be deciphered. Cotton knew he was on thin ice with the majority of ministers, and his words are festooned with qualifications and quibbles; and the other ministers also employ a medieval terminology that is at times nearly unintelligible to the modern reader. But you can make out some arguments and—more helpful still—the disputants cite particular Biblical sections whose relevance to their arguments is often quite clear.

Here's an example: Consider the Elders' Question 6 (page 47 of Hall): The Elders, who oppose Cotton on this matter (anticipating their criticism of Hutchinson), want to show that godly behavior is likely evidence that a person has received God's gift of grace. They ask Cotton: "Whether a Christian may maintain like constant comfort in his Soule, when he hath fallen into some grosse Sinne, or neglected some knowne Duty, as when he walked most closely with God?" [Translation: "Can one of the elect—a Christian— remain as confident ("maintain constant comfort in his soul") that he has received God's grace when he has done something awful ("fallen into some grosse sin") as when he behaved in a godly way?" By implication, should sinning make the saint worry that he was deluded in believing himself to have faith?]

Translated in the volatile context of 1636 Massachusetts: "Does our **behavior** offer a reliable index of the state of our souls?" Cotton's response appears on page 50: A Christian who misbehaves, Cotton answers, certainly won't find much emotional assurance and probably will be wracked with guilt ("the Spirit of God in him being grieved . . . it will not speak wonted *Peace* and *Comfort* to him.") But Cotton's additional words constitute a sharp rebuke to the elders: "Nevertheless, the assurance of a Christian mans good estate may be maintained to him, when the frame of his Spirit is growne much degenerate, *Isaiah 63.16*."

Cotton seems to be saying that God does not revoke His gift of grace because someone starts acting sinfully. A Christian saint (justified individual) will still go to heaven (his "good estate may be maintained to him") regardless of the person's behavior. God's gift of grace was not conditional on man's behavior; therefore, if one chosen for sainthood commits rape or murder, it must somehow accord with a plan that mortals simply cannot understand. It's not likely to happen, for grace should help the saint to obey God's law. Cotton claims that this idea is confirmed by Isaiah 63:16: "For thou art our Father, though Abraham does not know us, and Israel does not acknowledge us; thou, O Lord, art our Father, our Redeemer from of old is thy name." The story's context is the Israelites' persistence in sinfulness, which matters not to God, who still promises them redemption.

The Elders (that is to say, Anne's enemies) find this answer troubling. They say that they "much want satisfaction" (65) on the point. They worry that people will take this as an invitation to sin. Though a truly justified person cannot lose salvation, even if he has lapsed into recurrent sinfulness, they emphasize that this is not "God's usual course with his people" (66). In other words, if someone who thought that he had been saved fell into serious sins, he should seriously question whether or not he had really been saved in the first place. And it makes no sense, they add, that horrible sinners would "maintain Assurance of peace" (confidence that one has the gift of grace) "whilest they neglect to walk in the way of peace before him, P*salms 85.6.7.89; Galatians 6.16; 2 Samuel 12:13*.

2 Samuel 12:13 is cited as an example. King David, who is often cited as a paradigm, since he sins terribly but also repents, expresses anxiety about his condition: "David said to Nathan, 'I have sinned against the Lord.' And Nathan said to David, 'The Lord also has put away your sin; you shall not die.'" In citing this text, the Elders emphasize that even a great figure like David doesn't have "Assurance of peace" when he sins. Instead, he worries about the implications of his sins, even when Nathan can tell him definitively that God has "put away" his sin and won't damn him for it. If David could not be confident and assured of his salvation when he was sinning, how much more unlikely is it that an ordinary Christian will have such assurance when he has lapsed into recurrent sinfulness?

Strategy Advisory: Engagement with Theology. About half of each team (excluding the immigrants) should write a sermon on one or more points raised in the long exchanges in Chapter 3. Those who do not present longer papers (3-4 pages) can present one-page rebuttals. Bring Bibles to class, too. Your sermons will necessarily have some theoretical content and textual details (references to Biblical passages), but you should try to cast these ideas in terms that carry some measure of the emotional substance that prevailed 300 years ago.

Appendix B: Primary Documents

THE EXAMINATION OF MRS. ANNE HUTCHINSON AT THE COURT AT NEWTON

[Note: What follows is an account of Mrs. Anne Hutchinson's examination by the General Court in November 1637. It was reprinted by Charles Francis Adams as Antinomianism in the Colony of Massachusetts Bay, 1636-1638 *(1894) and has appeared more recently in the excellent document collection, David D. Hall, ed.,* The Antinomian Controversy, 1636-1638 *(Duke, 1990). The version below, edited by Elizabeth Shaw, Mark C. Carnes, and Michael P. Winship, differs from these in that, for purposes of clarity, the text has been occasionally altered or abridged. Editorial comments have been included in brackets.]*

November 1637
The Examination of Mrs. Anne Hutchinson at the court at Newtown.

Mr. Winthrop, governor. Mrs. Hutchinson, you are called here for troubling the peace of the commonwealth and the churches here; you are known to be a woman who has promoted and divulged troublesome opinions, and for joining in affinity and affection with some people whom the court had noticed and passed censure upon *[Wheelwright and his supporters; the Court had sentenced Wheelwright immediately before trying Hutchinson]*. We have been informed that you have spoken diverse things which are very prejudicial to the honor of the churches and their ministers, and you have maintained a meeting and an assembly in your house that has been condemned by the synod of churches assembly for being something not tolerable nor comely in the sight of God nor fitting for your sex, and regardless of previous complaints you have continued doing the same things.

Therefore we decided to send for you so that you can understand how things are, and that if you have acted wrongly we may reduce you so that you may become a profitable member here among us, otherwise if you will be obstinate in your course, to insure that you may trouble us no further.

Therefore I would ask you to state whether you have the opinions and are part of the factions that have already been handled in court, that is to say, whether or not you justify Mr. Wheelwright's sermon and the petition.

Mrs. Hutchinson. I am called here to answer before you but I hear no charges against me.

Gov. I have told you some already and can tell you more.

Mrs. H. Name one, Sir.

Gov. Have I not named some already?

Mrs. H. What have I said or done?

Gov. The things that you have done include that you harbored and countenanced those who are parties in the aforementioned faction.

Mrs. H. That's a mater of conscience, Sir.

Gov. You must keep your conscience or it must be kept for you.

Mrs. H. Must I not then entertain the saints because I must keep my conscience?

Gov. Say that one brother should commit felony or treason and come to his other brother's house; if the one who is harboring him knows him guilty and still conceals him then he is guilty of the same. So if you do countenance those that are transgressors of the law, you are also guilty.

Mrs. H. What law do they transgress?

Gov. The law of God and of the state.

Mrs. H. What in particular?

Gov. In particular because the Lord says honor thy father and thy mother.

Mrs. H. In entertaining those did I harbor them against any act or rule of God?

Gov. You knew that Mr. Wheelwright did preach this sermon and those that countenance him in this do break a law.

Mrs. H. What law have I broken?

Gov. Why, the fifth commandment [Honor your father and your mother; this commandment was considered to apply to rulers as well as parents].

Mrs. H. I deny that, for the things he said hold truth in the Lord.

Gov. You have joined with them in the faction.

Mrs. H. In what faction have I joined with them?

Gov. In presenting the petition [that Wheelwright's supporters gave to the General Court in March 1637].

Mrs. H. Suppose I had set my hand to the petition, what then?

Gov. You saw that case tried before.

Mrs. H. But I did not have my hand to the petition.

Gov. You have counseled them.

Mrs. H. Wherein?

Gov. Why, in entertaining them.

Mrs. H. What breach of law is that Sir?

Gov. Why, dishonoring of parents.

Mrs. H. But let us say Sir that I do fear the Lord and my parents, may not I entertain people that fear the Lord because my parents will not allow me?

Gov. If those who are prohibiting you are the fathers of the commonwealth, and those you are entertaining are of another religion, if you entertain them, then you dishonor your parents and are justly punishable.

Mrs. H. If I entertain them as they have dishonored their parents I do.

Gov. No, but you by countenancing them above others put honor upon them.

Mrs. H. I may put honor upon them as the children of God and as they do honor the Lord.

Gov. We do not mean to discourse with those of your sex but only to emphasize this; you do endeavor to set forward this faction and so you do dishonor us.

Mrs. H. I do not acknowledge any such thing, nor do I think that I ever dishonored you.

Gov. Why do you keep such a meeting at your house as you do every week upon a set day?

Mrs. H. It is lawful for me to do that, and you all do the same thing but you permit it for yourselves and condemn me for the same thing? The reason I started doing it was that when I first came to this land I did not go to meetings like those, and therefore it was assumed that I did not approve of such meetings but held them unlawful, and because of that assumption about me they said I was proud and did despise all ordinances. When they started saying that, a friend came to me and told me what was being said about me and therefore to prevent such opinions from being spread, I took it up, but there were meetings before I came; therefore I was not the first.

Gov. The last point you make is true. But if as you said, you hold meetings like we do, it would not have been offensive, but I will say that your meetings are not just of women alone, but have men in attendance as well.

Mrs. H. There was never any man with us.

Gov. Well, admit there was no man at your meeting and that you were sorry for it, there is no warrant for your doings, and by what warrant do you continue such a course?

Mrs. H. There lies a clear rule in Titus, that the elder women should instruct the younger and then I must have a time wherein I must do it.[1]

Gov. All this I grant you, I grant you a time for it, but for what reason should you, Mrs. Hutchinson, call a group from their other tasks to be taught by you?

Mrs. H. If you would please answer one question for me then I will willingly submit to any truth. If any come to my house to be instructed in the ways of God, what Scripture rule do I have to turn them away?

Gov. But if a hundred men came to you to be instructed, would you refuse them?

Mrs. H. I would if I thought I was breaking a Scripture rule.

Gov. Do you not see how you are breaking a rule here?

Mrs. H. No sir for my ground is they are men.

Gov. Men and women all is one for that, but suppose that a man should come and say: "Mrs. Hutchinson I hear that you are a woman who has the grace of God and you have knowledge in the word of God; I pray instruct me a little"—ought you not to instruct this man?

Mrs. H. I think I may— Do you think it not lawful for me to teach women, and why do you call me to teach the court?

Gov. We do not call you to teach the court but to reveal yourself.

Mrs. H. You have yet to tell me what rule allows me to send away those who seek my help and have peace in doing so.

Gov. You have to present a rule which justifies you in receiving them.

Mrs. H. I have done it.

Gov. I deny it because I have brought more arguments than you have.

Mrs. H. I say, to me it is a rule.

Mr. Endicot. You say that there are rules which you follow. But you contradict yourself. What rules do you follow here, only a custom in Boston?

Mrs. H. No Sir it is not my rule but a rule directly from Titus, and if you can convince me that it is not a rule I shall yield.

Gov. You know that rules cannot contradict each other, but this rule crosses that in the Corinthians.[2] But you must take it in this sense that elder women must instruct the younger about their business, and to love their husbands and not to make them to clash.

Mrs. H. I think that the rule in Corinthians is meant for publick times *[like church meetings]*.

Gov. Well, have you no more to say but this?

Mrs. H. I have said sufficient for my practice.

Gov. You may not continue in the way that you have in the past. We find your ways to be greatly prejudicial to the state. Besides, the meetings are dangerous because they may

---

[1] Titus 2:3-5: "The aged women . . . may teach the young women to be sober, to love their husbands, to love their children, to be discreet, chaste, keepers at home, good, obedient to their own husbands, that the word of God be not blasphemed."

[2] Perhaps 1 Corinthians 14:34, 35, "Let your women keep silence in the churches: for it is not permitted unto them to speak; but they are commanded to be under obedience, as also saith the law. And if they will learn any thing, let them ask their husbands at home: for it is a shame for women to speak in the church."

seduce honest people who arrive there because your opinions are obviously different from the word of God and so may seduce many simple souls that come to you for the meetings. Besides, the recent disturbances in the colony have come from none but those who have frequented your meetings, so that now they have flown off from the magistrates and ministers. Moreover, it does not agree with the commonwealth that families should be neglected by so many neighbors and women and so much time spent; we see no rule of God for this. We do not see that anyone should have authority to set up exercises besides what authority has already set up. So you will be guilty of the hurt that comes from this and we as well for permitting you to do so.

Mrs. H. Sir I do not believe that to be so.

Gov. Well, we see how it is, and we must restrain you from continuing in your former unlawful activities.

Mrs. H. If you have a rule for it from God's word you may.

Gov. We are your judges, and not you ours and we must compel you to it.

Mrs. H. If you will prohibit the meetings by your authority, I will freely let you because I am subject to your authority.

Mr. Simon Bradstreet. I would ask this question of Mrs. Hutchinson, whether you think this is lawful? For then this will follow that all other women that do not are in a sin.

Mrs. H. I conceive this is a free will offering.

Bradst. If it be a free will offering you ought to forbear it because it gives offence.

Mrs. H. Sir, I could forbear it myself but have not yet seen reasons that others must.

Bradst. I am not against all women's meetings but do think them to be lawful.

Mr. Dudley, dep gov. Here has been much spoken concerning Mrs. Hutchinson's meetings and among other answers, she has said that men do not come there. I would ask you this one question then, was there never any man at any of your meetings?

Gov. There are two meetings at their house.

Dep. Gov. What, there are two meetings?

Mrs. H. Yes Sir, there is a meeting of men and women and there is a meeting only for women.

Dep. Gov. Are they both constant?

Mrs. H. No, occasionally they do not meet.

Mr. Endicot. Is it only men who teach the men's meetings or do not women sometimes?

Mrs. H. Never as I heard, not one.

Dep. Gov. I would go a little higher with Mrs. Hutchinson. About three years ago, we were all in peace. From the time that Mrs. Hutchinson arrived, she has made a disturbance. Some that came over with her in her ship complained to me of her as soon as they landed *[Dudley was governor that year]*. I asked the pastor and teacher of Boston to enquire of her, and afterwards I was satisfied that she held no opinions different from us. But within just half a year after, she had begun to express her strange opinions and had made parties in the country, and finally it came out that Mr. Cotton and Mr. Vane shared her opinions, but now Mr. Cotton has cleared himself of that charge and he is not of that mind. But now it appears that because of her meeting that Mrs. Hutchinson has taken hold of the minds of many so that she seems to have a potent party in the country. Now if all these things that have endangered us are from her meetings, and if she in particular has disparaged all the ministers in the land charging that they have preached a covenant of works, and only Mr. Cotton a covenant of grace, we cannot tolerate this. Therefore having driven to the foundation of the problem and finding that Mrs. Hutchinson is the one that depraved all the ministers and caused the problem, if we remove she that is the root of the problem, we will be able to eradicate it entirely.

Mrs. H. I pray Sir prove that I said that they preached nothing but a covenant of works.

Dep.Gov. [Well perhaps you didn't say the exact words . . .] Why, a Jesuit may preach truth sometimes.

Mrs. H. Did I ever say they preached a covenant of works then?

Dep. Gov. If they do not preach a covenant of grace clearly, then they preach a covenant of works.

Mrs. H. No Sir, one may preach a covenant of grace more clearly than another, so I said.

D. Gov. We are not upon that now but upon position.

Mrs. H. Prove this then, Sir, what you say I said.

D. Gov. When they do preach a covenant of works, do they preach truth?

Mrs. H. Yes Sir, but when they preach a covenant of works for salvation, that is not truth.

D. Gov. I do but ask you this, when the ministers do preach a covenant of works, do they preach a way of salvation?

Mrs. H. I did not come hither to answer to questions of that sort.

D. Gov. Because you will deny the thing.

Mrs. H. Yes, but that is to be proved first.

D. Gov. I will make it plain that you did say that the ministers did preach a covenant of works.

Mrs. H. I deny that.

D. Gov. And that you said they were not able ministers of the new testament, but only Mr. Cotton is.

Mrs. H. If ever I spake that, I proved it by God's word.

Court. Very well, very well.

Mrs. H. : If one shall come unto me in private and desire me seriously to tell them what I thought of such a minister, I must either speak false or true in my answer.

D. Gov. Likewise I will prove this, that you said the gospel in the letter and words holds forth nothing but a covenant of works and that all that do not agree with you are in a covenant of works.

Mrs. H. : I deny this, for if I should so say I should speak against my own judgment.

Mr. Endicot. I desire to speak, seeing Mrs. Hutchinson seems to lay something against the ministers that are to witness against her.

Gov. I have one thing to add. The court notices that Mrs. Hutchinson can tell when to speak and when to hold her tongue. When we ask her a question, she desires to be pardoned *[i.e., she spoke her mind to the ministers, but she will not tell us what she thinks]*.

Mrs. H. It is one thing for me to come before a public magistracy and there to speak what they would have me to speak and another when a man comes to me in a way of friendship privately.

Gov. What if the *[subject]* matter be all one?

Mr. Hugh Peters [minister]. We ministers are reluctant to speak unless the court commands us. Then we shall answer to Mrs. Hutchinson.

Gov. This speech was not spoken in a corner but in a public assembly, and though these things were spoken in private, now that they are coming to us, we are to deal with them as public.

Mr. Peters. We shall give you a fair account of what was said. We hope that we are not to be considered as informers against the gentlewoman, but we give a brief account as it might serve for our country and posterity to do so. This gentlewoman fell under suspicion from her landing in Boston, that she was not only difficult in her opinions, but also of an intemperate spirit. I do not remember well what happened at her landing *[Peters came a year later]*, but I do remember that this controversy began as soon as Mr. Vane and ourselves came, and it did reflect upon Mrs. Hutchinson. Some of our brethren had dealt with her, and as a result, some of our ministry suffers as if we had been teaching a covenant of works instead of a covenant of grace *[unlike John Cotton]*.

Upon these and similar troubles, we spoke to Mr. Cotton. The General Court that was meeting was aware of these problems, and since we understood that this gentlewoman was a chief agent in these troubles, our desire to Mr. Cotton was to tell us wherein the difference lay between him and us, for the spring of this comparison between him and us arose, as we thought, from this gentlewoman, and so we told him. Mr Cotton said that he thought it not according to God to bring this to the magistrates, but to take some other course of action.

Going on in the conversation, we thought it good to send for this gentlewoman, and she willingly came. At the very first, we told her that there were reports that she thought our ministry to be different from the ministry of the gospel, and that we taught a covenant of works, etc, and that this was her table talk. Therefore we desired her to clear herself and deal plainly. She was very tender at the first. Some of our brethren did desire proof, and she responded that 'The fear of man is a snare why should I be afraid.' *[Proverbs 29-25]* These were her words. So I asked her this question: 'What difference do you find between your teacher and us?' She did not ask us to preserve her from danger or that we should be silent.

She told me there was a wide and broad difference between our brother Mr. Cotton and ourselves. I desired to know the difference. She answered that he preaches the covenant of grace, and you are not able ministers to the New Testament and know no more than the apostles did before the resurrection of Christ. I then asked her, 'What did you conceive of such a brother?' She answered that he had not the seal of the spirit. And we asked her other questions but her substance was that she believed that we were not able ministers of the gospel.

And after that day was over, our brother Cotton was sorry that she should put us under a covenant of works and wished she had not done so. The Boston elders were present there and we put them in charge of handling her, and Mr. Cotton said they would speak further with her, and after some time she answered that we were gone as far as the apostles were before Christ's ascension. And since that we have gone with tears, some of us, to her.

Mrs. H. If our pastor would show his writings you should see what I said and that many things are not as it is reported.

Mr. Wilson [minister]. Sister Hutchinson, about the writings of which you speak, I do not have them, and I did not write down all that was said that day, yet what was recorded I will avouch.

Dep. Gov. I desire that the other elders will say what Mrs. Peters said.

Mr. Weld [minister]. Being desired by the honored court, that which our brother Peters had spoken was the truth and that he has accurately recounted the things that were said. And I asked her why she cast such criticisms upon the ministers of the country; though we were poor sinful men, we cared not for ourselves but were distressed to hear our precious doctrine so blasphemed. She was sparing in her speech. I need not repeat the things that have been truly related.

She said the fear of man is a snare, and therefore said she would speak freely and she spoke her judgment and mind freely as was before related, that Mr. Cotton did preach a covenant of grace and we a covenant of works. And this I remember, she said we could not preach a covenant of grace because we were not sealed, and we were not able ministers of the new testament, no more than were the disciples before the resurrection of Christ.

Mr. Phillips [minister]. For my own part, I have had little to do with these things. Only at that time I was there. I was not then privy to the background which our brother Peters has mentioned. They simply asked me to accompany them while they dealt with her. At

The Trial of Anne Hutchinson

first she was unwilling to answer but finally said there was a great deal of difference between ourselves and Mr. Cotton. Upon this, Mr. Cotton did say that he wished that she had not said that. Being asked for specifics, she claimed that Mr. Shephard did not preach a covenant of grace clearly, and she instanced our brother Weld. Then I asked her of myself (since she spoke rashly of them all) because she never heard me at all. She likewise said that we were not able ministers of the new testament, and her reason was because we were not sealed.

Mr. Simmes [minister]. For my own part, being called to speak in this case to discharge my responsibility to the commonwealth and to God, I shall speak briefly. I had no acquaintance with Mrs. Hutchinson in our native country but was in her company twice before arriving here, where I did perceive that she did criticize ministers. But I came along with her in the ship, and while we were in the great cabin together those listening did agree with the sermons of Mr. Lothrop and myself. Only there was a secret opposition to things being preached. The main source of conflict was about demonstrating assurance of salvation, and also controversial was that place in John concerning the love of the brethren *[did sanctification, as demonstrated by loving one's fellow Christians, prove that you were saved]*[3]. I took notice of the corruptness and narrowness of her opinions. She also said that when she came to Boston there would be something more to be see than I said, for such speeches were cast about and abused as that of our savior, I have many things to say but you cannot bear them now *[John 16. 2]*. And later when we had arrived, she desired to be admitted as a member of the church. My presence was requested, and then I was satisfied by Mr. Cotton's questioning of her. And for things which have been recounted today, as far as I can remember they are the truth, and when I asked her what she thought of me, she said 'alas you know my mind long ago,' yet I do not consider myself disparaged by her testimony and I would not trouble the court.

Mr. Wilson. I desire you would permit me to speak regarding statements made about her entrance into the church. There was some difficulty made, but she answered to the full satisfaction of our teacher and myself. She did not deny that sanctification could demonstrate justification, but only justification must be first. Our teacher told her then that if that was her opinion she would take away the scruple: for we thought that matter, for point of order we did not greatly stand upon, because we hoped she would hold with us in that truth as well as the other.

Mr. Shephard. I am loath to speak in this assembly concerning this gentlewoman in question, but I must speak my conscience. There have been many complaints in this country of our ministry. This is my opinion on those complaints: let men speak what they will not only against persons but against the ministry. We should let that pass, but let us strive to speak to the consciences of men, knowing that if we have the truth with us, we shall not need to prove our words by our practice and our ministry to the hearts of the people. Our words should speak for us, and therefore I have satisfied my brethren and myself with that point.

Now regarding this gentlewoman, I do not remember every particular, but I do remember that the goal of our meeting was to satisfy ourselves in some points. Mrs. Hutchinson was desired to speak her thoughts concerning the ministers of the Bay. Now I remember that

---

[3] I John 4.21 "And this commandment have we from him, That he who loveth God love his brother also"

she said that we were not able ministers of the new testament. I asked her for details. She gave the example of hearing me preach when I gave some means whereby a Christian might come to the assurance of God's love. She instanced that I was not sealed and I asked her to justify her claim. She said 'because you put love for an evidence.' Now I am sure she was wrong because if assurance is a holy estate, there must be plenty of the graces of holiness to evidence it.

Mr. Eliot [minister]. I am loath to spend time, therefore I confirm what has been said already. Our brethren asked us to write and I did write a few things, the substance of which hath been here spoken and I have it in writing; therefore I do avouch it.

Mr. Shephard. I desire to say that it may be but a slip of her tongue, and I hope she will be sorry for it, and then we shall be glad of it.

Dep. Gov. I called these witnesses, Mrs. Hutchinson. They have proved their claims, and yet you deny them. You said they preached a covenant of works and that they were not able ministers of the new testament. There are two other things that you claimed which were that the Scriptures in the letter of them held forth nothing but a covenant of works and likewise that those that were under a covenant of works cannot be saved.

Mrs. H. Prove that I said so.

Gov. Did you say so?

Mrs. H. No, Sir, it is your conclusion.

Dep. Gov. Why do I ask you if you if you deny what is so fully proven?

Gov. Here are six undeniable ministers who say it is true, and yet you deny that you did say that they did preach a covenant of works and that they were not able ministers of the gospel. It appears plainly that you have spoken it, and whereas you say that it was drawn from you in a way of friendship, you also said that it was out of conscience that you said 'The fear of man is a snare wherefore should I be afraid, I will speak plainly and freely.'

Mrs. H. I absolutely deny that. This is how I answered the first question that they asked. They thought that I conceived there was a difference between them and Mr. Cotton. At the first I was somewhat reserved, then said Mr. Peters 'I pray answer the question directly as fully and as plainly as you would desire that we should tell you our minds. Mrs. Hutchinson, we come for plain dealing and telling you our hearts.' Then I said I would deal as plainly as I could, and although they claim that I said they were under a covenant of works and like the apostles, why those two speeches contradict each other . . . I might say they might preach a covenant of works as did the apostles, but to preach a covenant of works and be under a covenant of works is another business.

Dep. Gov. There have been six witnesses to prove this and yet you deny it.

Mrs. H. I deny that these were the first words that were spoken.

Gov. You make the case worse, for you clearly demonstrated that you were opening your mind not to satisfy them but to satisfy your own conscience.

Mr. Peters. We do not want to be so narrow to the court and to the gentlewoman about chronology, the important fact is that it was said.

Dep Gov. As for the letter of scripture holding forth nothing but a covenant of works, and that we are in a state of damnation, being under a covenant of works, you also deny those two things. Now the case stands thus. About three quarters of a year ago I heard of it, and someone who is not present here today but will affirm what I am to say, came to me stating that he did hear you say it in so many words *[Nathaniel Ward, who was at the meeting with the other ministers].* He wrote it and signed it and I can produce it when the court pleases.

Gov. How do you respond Mrs. Hutchinson? Though nothing is directly proved, yet you hear it may be.

Mrs. H. I acknowledge using the words of the apostle to the Corinthian to him, that they that were ministers of the letter and not the spirit did preach a covenant of works. When he argued that there was no such scripture, I fetched the Bible and showed him this place 2 Cor 3:6.[4] He said that was the letter of the law. No said I, it is the letter of the gospel.

Gov. You have already stated this.

Mrs. H. Then upon further discussion about assurance of salvation and holding it out by the manifestation of the Holy Spirit *[Cotton's way]*, he did acknowledge that to be the nearest way, but yet said he, will you not acknowledge that which we hold forth to be a way too wherein we may have hope; no truly if that be a way it is a way to hell.

Gov. Mrs. Hutchinson, the court has labored to make you acknowledge the error of your way so that you may be reduced, but it is late and we shall therefore give you a little more time to consider what has been said here today and we desire that you attend the court again in the morning.

The Next Morning

Gov. Last night we proceeded as far as we could in the hearing of the case against Mrs. Hutchinson. She was accused of diverse things, her ordinary meetings about religious exercises, her speeches in criticism of the ministers among us, and the weakening of the hands and hearts of the people towards them. Here was sufficient proof given regarding the accusations against her concerning the ministers and their ministry, as that she stated that they did preach a covenant of works when others did preach a covenant of grace, and that they were not able ministers of the new testament, and that they had not the seal of the spirit. She spoke these things not spoken in the spirit of a private conference, but out of conscience. She alleged warrant from scripture, the fear of man is a snare and seeing God had given her a calling she would speak freely. Some other speeches she used, as that the letter of the scripture held forth a covenant of works, and this is offered to be proved by probable grounds. If there be anything else that the court has to say they may speak.

Mrs. H. The ministers come in their own cause. Now the Lord has said that an oath is the end of all controversy; and although there are a sufficient number of witnesses, yet they are not testifying under oath, therefore I request they speak under oath.

Gov. Well, the court has jurisdiction to decide whether or not they will speak an oath, and this case is not the same as in case of a jury. If they are satisfied without the oath, then they have enough matter to proceed.

Mrs. H. Since yesterday, I went home and perused some notes out of what Mr. Wilson wrote and I find things not to be as has been alleged.

Gov. Where are the writings?

Mrs. H. I do not have them. It may be Mr. Wilson has them.

Gov. What are the instructions that you can give, Mr. Wilson?

Mr. Wilson. I do say that Mr. Vane desired for me to write the discourse out, and whether he has it or someone else does, I do not know. My own copy is somewhat imperfect, but I could make it perfect with a little pains.

Gov. In response to that which you allege as an objection against the elders, Mrs. Hutchinson, it is vain and untrue, for they are not prosecutors in this cause but are called as witnesses in the cause.

Mrs. H. But they are witnesses of their own cause.

---

[4] "Who also hath made us able ministers of the new testament; not of the letter, but of the spirit: for the letter killeth, but the spirit giveth life."

Gov. It is not their cause but the cause of the whole country, and they were unwilling that it should come forth, but that it was the glory and honor of God.

Mrs. H. But it is the Lord's ordinance that an oath should be the end of all strife, therefore they are to deliver what they do upon oath.

Mr. Bradstreet. Mrs. Hutchinson, these are but circumstances and adjuncts to the cause. Suppose that they make a mistake about what you said, then you will cause them to sin if you insist that they testify under oath.

Mrs. H. That is not the thing. If they accuse me I desire it may be upon oath.

Gov. If the court be not satisfied they may have an oath.

Mr. Nowel. It would be convenient if the country were also satisfied because I hear it affirmed that things which were spoken in private are carried abroad to the publick, and thereupon they do undervalue the ministers of the congregations.

Mr. Brown. I desire to speak. If I am not mistaken an oath is of a high nature, and it is not to be taken unless there is a controversy. For my part I am afraid of an oath and fear that we shall take God's name in vain if we insist on an oath, for we may take the testimony of these men without an oath.

Mr. Endicot. I think the ministers are so well-known to us that we do not need for them to take an oath. But indeed an oath is the end of all strife.[5]

Mrs. H. There are some that will take their oaths to the contrary.

Mr. Endicot. Then it will be called a controversy, therefore we desire to see the notes and know who will swear.

Gov. Let those not satisfied in the court speak.

Many. We are not satisfied.

Gov. I would speak to Mrs. Hutchinson. If the ministers shall take an oath, will you sit down satisfied?

Mrs. H. I can't be satisfied against my own conscience, notwithstanding oaths.

Mr. Stoughton. I am fully satisfied that the ministers do speak the truth, but in regard of censure I dare not hold up my hand to that because it is a course of justice, and I cannot satisfy myself to proceed so far in a way of justice, and therefore I should desire an oath in this as in all other things. I do but speak to prevent offence if I should not hold up my hand at the censure unless there be an oath given.

Mr. Peters. We are ready to swear if we see a way of God in it.

(Here was a parley between the deputy governor and Mr. Stoughton about the oath.)

Mr. Endicot. If they will not be satisfied with a testimony, an oath will be in vain.

Mr. Stoughton. I am persuaded that Mrs. Hutchinson and many other godly-minded people will be satisfied without an oath.

Mrs. H. An oath, Sir, is an end of all strife, and it is God's ordinance.

Mr. Endicot. It is a sign what respect she hath to their words, and further, pray see your argument, you will have the words that were written, and yet Mr. Wilson says he writ not all, and now you will not believe all these godly ministers without an oath.

Mrs. H. Mr. Wilson affirmed that what he gave to the governor was true.

Some reply. But not all the truth.

Mr. Wilson. I did say so far as I did take them they were true.

---

[5] Hebr. 6.16: "For men verily sweare by the greater, and an oath for confirmation is to them an end of all strife."

The Trial of Anne Hutchinson

Mr. Harlakenden. I would like for the spectators to note that the court trusts the evidence that has been presented, although we see that whatever evidence that is presented will not satisfy, because they are resolved upon giving the thing and therefore I think you will not be unwilling to give your oaths.

Gov. I see no need for an oath in this thing because it is true and the substance of the matter has been confirmed by diverse. Yet in order to satisfy everyone, if the elders will agree to take an oath they shall have it given them.

Dep Gov. Let us combine things so that Mrs. Hutchinson may see what they have their oaths for.

Mrs. H. I will prove by what Mr. Wilson has written that they never heard me say such a thing.

Mr. Sims. We desire to have the paper and have it read.

Mr. Harlakenden. I am persuaded that the elders speak the truth, and therefore I do not see it necessary to call them to oath.

Gov. We cannot charge any thing of untruth upon them.

Mr. Harlakenden. Besides, Mrs. Hutchison says that they are not able ministers of the new testament.

Mrs. H. They do not need to swear to that.

Dep. Gov. Will you confess it then.

Mrs. H. I will not deny it nor say it.

Dep. Gov. You must do one.

Mrs. H. After they have taken an oath, I will make good what I say.

Gov. Let us state the case and then we may know what to do. That which Mrs. Hutchinson is accused of is this, that she has traduced the magistrates and ministers of this jurisdiction, that she has said that the ministers preached a covenant of works and Mr. Cotton a covenant of grace and that they were not able ministers of the gospel. She excuses it by claiming that she made it a private conference and with a promise of secrecy, etcetera. Now she was charged with all this, and the ministers therefore sent for her, seeing she made it her table talk, and then she said the fear of man was a snare and therefore she would not be frightened of them.

Mrs. H. I desire that they may take their oaths upon the words that you just spoke.

Gov. What we would ask of the reverend elders is to deliver upon oath that which they can remember themselves.

Mr. Shepard. I see no reason for an oath, except the importunity of this gentlewoman.

Mr. Endicot. You lifted up your eyes as if you took God to witness that you came to entrap none, and yet you will have them swear.

Mr. Harlakenden. Put any passage unto them and see what they say.

Mrs. H. They say I said the fear of man is a snare, why should I be afraid. When I came before them and they were asking me many things, I was backward to answer at first, finally I thought of this scripture: 29[th]Prov.15. The fear of man bringeth a snare, but whoso putteth his trust in the Lord shall be safe.

Mr. Harlakenden. This is not an essential thing.

Gov. I remember his testimony was this.

Mrs. H. Aye, that was the thing that I deny, because they were my words and they were not spoken at the beginning as they have said.

Mr. Peters. We cannot tell what was first or last, and we suppose that an oath is an end of all strife, and we are tender of it, yet the main thing against her is that she charged us to be unable ministers of the gospel and to preach a covenant of works.

Gov. You do understand that the court is clear, for we are all satisfied that you speak truth, but because to ease all scruples, we desire that you would satisfy the spectators by your oath.

Mr. Bishop. I desire to know before they are put to oath whether their testimony is valid.

Dep. Gov. Why do you trouble the court with such questions? Notice the emphasis that Mrs. Hutchinson makes of the fact that she had witnesses to disprove what was said, and here is no man to bear witness.

Mrs. H. If you will not call them, that is nothing to me.

Mr. Eliot. We want to know of her and her witnesses and what they deny, and then we will speak under oath. I know nothing we have spoken of but we may swear to.

Mr. Sims. Yes, and more than we have spoken to.

Mr. Stoughton. I would be glad that an oath should be given that so the person to be condemned should be satisfied in her conscience, and I would say the same for my own conscience if I should join in the censure—[*Two or thee lines in the MS are not legible*].

Mr. Coggeshall. I desire to speak a word—it is desired that the elders would confer with Mr. Cotton before they swear.

Gov. Shall we not believe so many godly elders in a cause wherein we know the mind of the party without their testimony?

Mr. Endicot to Mr. Coggeshall. I will tell you what I say. I think that this carriage of yours tends to further casting dirt upon the face of the judges.

Mr. Harlakenden. Her carriage does the same because she does not object any essential thing, but she goes upon circumstances and yet would have them sworn.

Mrs. H. This I would say to them. Since it was affirmed by Deputy-Governor Dudley that he would bring proof of these things, and the elders bring proof in their own cause, I still desire that particular witnesses be [*put under oath*] for these things that they speak.

Gov. The elders know what an oath is, and as it is an ordinance of God, it should be used as one.

Mrs. H. That is what I desire, and because the deputy spoke of witnesses I have witnesses of my own here present.

Mr. Colborn. We desire that our teacher may be called to speak.

(Upon this, Mr. Cotton came and sat down by Mrs. Hutchinson)

Mr. Endicot. This would cast some blame upon the ministers. Well, but whatever he will say, we will believe the ministers.

Mr. Eliot and Mr. Shepard. We wish to know why we should take an oath.

Mr. Stoughton. Because it is an end of all strife, and I think you ought to just swear and put an end to the matter.

Mr. Peters. Our oath is not to satisfy Mrs. Hutchinson but to satisfy the court.

Mr. Endicot. The assembly will be satisfied by it.

Dep. Gov. If the country will not be satisfied, you must swear.

Mr. Shepard. I don't think that the country requires it.

Dep. Gov. Let her witnesses be called.

Gov. Who are they?

Mrs. H. Mr. Leveret and our teacher and Mr. Coggeshall.

Gov. Mr. Coggeshall was not present.

Mr. Coggeshall. Yes, I was present, but I decided not to speak up about it until I was called.

Gov. Will you, Mr. Coggeshall, refute the previous testimonies?

Mr. Coggeshall. Yes I dare say that she did not say all that which they lay against her.

Mr. Peters. How dare you look into the court to make that statement?

Mr. Coggeshall. Mr. Peters takes it upon himself to forbid me to speak. I shall be silent.

Mr. Stoughton. Aye, but she intended this that they say.

Gov. Well, Mr. Leveret, what were the words? Please speak.

Mr. Leveret. To my best remembrance, when the elders did send for her, Mr. Peters did vehemently urge her state the difference between Mr. Cotton and them, and upon his

The Trial of Anne Hutchinson

urging of her she said the fear of man is a snare, but they that trust upon the Lord shall be safe. And so when they asked her to explain the differences, she answered that they did not preach a covenant of grace so clearly as Mr. Cotton did, and she gave this reason of it because that as the apostles were for a time without the spirit, so until they had received the witness of the spirit they could not preach a covenant of grace clearly.

Gov. Don't you remember that she said they were not able ministers of the new testament?

Mrs. H. Mr. Weld and I conversed for an hour at the window and then I said that, if I said it.

Mr. Weld. Will you affirm that in the court? Did I not say that to you, Mrs. Hutchinson, before the elders. When I produced the thing, you then called for proof. Was not my answer to you, leave it there, and if I cannot prove it, you shall be blameless?

Mrs. H. That is what I remembered saying, do you not remember that I came afterwards to the window when you were writing and there spoke to you?

Mr. Weld. No truly.

Mrs. H. But I do very well.

Gov. Mr. Cotton, the court desires that you declare what you do remember of the conference which is now in question.

Mr. Cotton. I did not think I should be called as a witness and therefore I did not labour to recall what was done; but the greatest passage that took impression upon me was to this purpose. The elders said that they had heard that she had spoken some condemning words of their ministry, and, among other things, they did first ask her to answer in what way she thought their ministry differed from mine, I don't know how the comparison sprang, but I was sorry that any comparison should be between me and my brethren and it was uncomfortable.

She told them that they did not hold forth a covenant of grace as I did, but wherein did we differ? She said they did not hold forth the seal of the spirit as he doth. They ask, where is the difference there? Why, said she, speaking to one or other of them, I do not know to whom, you preach of the seal of the spirit upon a work and he upon free grace without a work or without respect to a work. He preaches the seal of the spirit upon free grace and you upon a work.

I told her I was sorry that she had compared my ministry and theirs, for she had said more than I could myself, and I would have rather that she put us in fellowship with them and not have made that discrepancy. She said, she found the difference. Then there were some speeches upon the thing and I remember I gave the example of the story of Thomas Bilney in John Fox's book of martyrs, how freely the spirit witnessed unto him without any respect to a work, as he claimed. Now from this sprang other speeches.

If you put me in mind of any thing I shall speak it, but this was the sum of the difference, nor did it seem to be so ill taken as it is, and our brethren did say also that they could not so easily believe reports as they had done and withal mentioned that they would speak no more of it, some of them did; and afterwards some of them did say they were less satisfied than before. And I must say that I did not find her saying that they were under a covenant of works, nor that she said they did preach a covenant of works.

Gov. You say you do not remember but can you say she did not speak so … *[here two lines of the original text were defaced.]*

Mr Cotton. I do remember that she looked at them as the apostles before the ascension.

Mr. Peters. I humbly desire to remind our reverend teacher. Perhaps it will help him to remember how this came in. Do you not remember that she said we were not sealed with the spirit of grace, therefore could not preach a covenant of grace, and that she said that we may preach it in our judgment but not in experience, but she clearly said that we were not sealed.

Mr. Cotton. You do cause me to remember that she was asked why cannot we preach a covenant of grace? Why, saith she, because you can preach no more than you know, or to that purpose, she spoke. Now that she said you could not preach a covenant of grace, I do not remember such a thing. I remember well that she said you were not sealed with the seal of spirit.

Mr. Peters. There was a double seal found out that day which never was.

Mr. Cotton. I know very well that she took the seal of the spirit in that sense for the full assurance of God's favour, by the holy ghost, and now that place in the Ephesians doth hold out that seal.[6]

Mr. Peters.... [missing text]

Mr. Cotton. Under favor, I do not remember that.

Mr. Peters. Therefore her answer clears it in your judgment but not in your experience [her answer makes sense to you, but you did not hear her say it].

Mrs. H. My name is precious, and you do affirm a thing which I utterly deny.

D. Gov. You should have brought the book with you.

Mr. Nowell. The witnesses do not answer that which you ask.

Gov. I do not see that we need their testimony any further. Mr. Cotton has expressed what he remembered and what made an impression on him, and so I think that the other elders also remembered what made an impression upon them.

Mr. Weld. Then I said to Mrs. Hutchinson when it had come to this issue, why did you let us go so long and never tell us of it?

Gov. I wonder why the elders *[from the other churches]* should request the elders of our congregation to have dealt with her if they did not have any cause.

Mr. Cotton. Brother Weld and Brother Shepard, I then cleared myself to you that I understood her when she expressed that you held forth something in your preaching that was not pertinent to the seal of the spirit....*[two lines have been defaced]*.

Dep. Gov. They affirm that Mrs. Hutchinson did say they were not able ministers of the new testament.

Mr. Cotton. I do not remember it.

Mrs. H. If you permit me, I will relate what I know to be true. Being much troubled to see the falseness of the constitution of the church of England, I was on the verge of turning separatist [7]; but at that point I kept a day of solemn humiliation and pondering of the issue; this scripture was brought to my mind--he that denies Jesus Christ to become in the flesh is antichrist[8]--I considered this and in considering it found that the papists did not deny Him to be come in the flesh, nor did we deny Him---who then was antichrist? Was the Turk antichrist only? The Lord knows that I could not discover the meaning of scripture; He must by his prophetical office open it to me.

---

[6] Eph. 1.13, "In whom ye also trusted, after that ye heard the word of trueth, the Gospel of your salvation: in whom also after that yee believed, yee were sealed with that holy Spirit of promise."

[7] Separatists were puritans who had given up on the Church of England and formed illegal completely separate and independent churches. The pilgrims who founded Plymouth colony were separatists.

[8] I John 4.3, "And every spirit that confesseth not that Jesus Christ is come in the flesh is not of God: and this is that spirit of antichrist, whereof ye have heard that it should come; and even now already is it in the world."

The Trial of Anne Hutchinson

So after that being unsatisfied, the Lord was pleased to bring this scripture out of the Hebrews. He that denies the testament denies the testator, and in this did open unto me and give me to see that those which did not teach the new covenant had the spirit of antichrist, and upon this he discovered the ministry unto me and ever since.[9] I bless the Lord, he has let me see which was the clear ministry and which the wrong.

Since that time I confess I have been more choice and he hath let me to distinguish between the voice of my beloved and the voice of Moses, the voice of John Baptist and the voice of antichrist, for all those voices are spoken of in scripture. Now if you do condemn me for speaking what in my conscience I know to be truth, I must commit myself unto the Lord.

Mrs. Nowell. How do you know that it was the Holy Spirit speaking to you?

Mrs. H. How did Abraham know that it was God that bid him offer his son, being a breach of the six commandment?[10]

Dep. Gov. By an immediate voice.

Mrs. H. Also for me it was an immediate revelation.

Dep. Gov. How! An immediate revelation.

Mrs. H. By the voice of his own spirit to my soul. I will give you another scripture, Jer. 46.27.28[11] out of which the Lord showed me what he would do for me and the rest of his servants. But after he was pleased to reveal himself to me I did presently like Abraham run to Hagar.[12] And after that he did let me see the atheism of my own heart for which I begged of the Lord that it might not remain in my heart. And being thus, he did show me this (a twelvemonth after) which I told you of before.

Ever since that time I have been confident of what he hath revealed unto me. [text missing] another place out of Daniel chap. 7. and he and for [text missing] us all, wherein he shewed me the sitting of the judgment and the standing of all high and low before the Lord and how thrones and kingdoms were cast down before him.

When our teacher came to New England it was a great trouble unto me, since my brother [in-law] Wheelwright was also removed from his ministry. I was then much troubled concerning the ministry under which I lived, and then the place in the 30th of Isaiah [verse 20] was brought to my mind. Though the Lord give thee bread of adversity and water of affliction, yet shall not thy teachers be removed into corners any more, but thine eyes shall see thy teachers.

The Lord giving me this promise, and they being gone, there was none then left that I was able to hear, and I could not be at rest, but I must come hither. Yet that place of Isaiah did much follow me, though the Lord give thee the bread of adversity and water of affliction.

---

[9] Hutchinson is fusing 1 John 4.3 (above) with Hebrews 9.16, "For where a testament is, there must also of necessity be the death of the testator."

[10] The story of Abraham's divinely aborted sacrifice of his son is in Genesis 22.

[11] "But fear not thou, O my servant Jacob, and be not dismayed, O Israel: for, behold, I will save thee from afar off, and thy seed from the land of thy captivity; and Jacob shall return, and be in rest and at ease, and none shall make *him* afraid. Fear thou not, O Jacob my servant, saith the Lord: for I *am* with thee; for I will make a full end of all the nations whither I have driven thee; but I will not make a full end of thee, but correct thee in measure: yet will I not leave thee wholly unpunished."

[12] Hutchinson means that she turned to a covenant of works, Hagar standing for that covenant in puritan interpretations of the Bible, with Gal. 4 as their justification

This place lying, I say, upon me, then this place in Daniel *[6.4,5]* was brought to me and showed me that though I should meet with affliction, yet I am the same God that delivered Daniel out of the lion's den. I will also deliver thee *[text possibly omitted.]* Therefore, I desire you to look to it, for you see this scripture fulfilled this day, and therefore I desire you that as you regard the Lord and the church and commonwealth to consider and look what you do. You have power over my body, but the Lord Jesus has power over my body and soul, and assure yourselves this much: you do as much as in you lies to put the Lord Jesus Christ from you, and if you go on in this course you begin, you will bring a curse upon you and your posterity, and the mouth of the Lord has spoken it.

Dep. Gov. What is the scripture she brings?

Mr. Stoughton. Behold I turn away from you.

Mrs.H. But now having seen him which is invisible, I do not fear what man can do to me.[13]

Gov. Daniel was delivered by miracle. Do you think that you will be delivered so too?

Mrs. H. I do here speak it before the court. I look that the Lord should deliver me by his providence.

Mr. Harlakenden. I may read scripture and the most glorious hypocrite may read them and yet go down to hell.

Mrs. H. It may be so.

Mr. Bartholomew. I remind Mrs. Hutchinson of one thing. She was aware that I knew of her opinions because she had been at my house in London. On the boat over, therefore, she was afraid or reluctant to share them with me. But when she had her first sight of Boston and looking at the meanness of the place, I conceive, she uttered these words, if she had not a sure word that England should be destroyed, her heart would shake. Now it seemed to me at that time very strange that she said that.

Mrs. H. I do not remember that I looked upon the meanness of the place nor did it discourage me, because I knew the bounds of my habitations were determined, etcetera.

Mr. Bartholomew. I speak as a member of the court. I fear that her revelations will deceive.

Gov. Have you heard of any of her revelations?

Mr. Bartholomew. I am sorry to see her here now, and I have nothing against her. The things that I said were only to discover of what manner of spirit she was; and I remember as we were going through Paul's churchyard she was very inquisitive after revelations and said that she had never had any great thing done about her but it was revealed to her beforehand.

Mrs. H. I say the same thing again.

Mr. Bartholomew. And also that she said that she was come to New-England only for Mr. Cotton's sake. As for Mr. Hooker (as I remember) she said she did not like his spirit, only she spoke of a sermon of his in the low countries *[the Netherlands]* wherein he said thus—it was revealed to me yesterday that England should be destroyed.[14] She took notice of that passage and it was very acceptable to her.

Mr. Cotton. Let me ask one thing of you to remember, Mr. Bartholomew, that you never spoke to me.

---

[13] Hebrew 11.27, " By faith he forsook Egypt, not fearing the wrath of the king: for he endured, as seeing him who is invisible."

[14] This sermon was published as *The Danger of Desertion* (London, 1641).

The Trial of Anne Hutchinson

Mr. Barth. No sir, I never spoke of it to you and therefore I desire to clear Mr. Cotton.

Gov. There needs no more of that.

Mr. Barth. Only I remember her eldest daughter said in the ship that she had a revelation that a young man in the ship should be saved, but he must walk in the ways of her mother.

Mr. Sims. I could say something to that purpose, for she said—then what would you say if we should be at New England within these three weeks, and I reproved her vehemently for it.

Mr. Eliot. That speech of Mr. Hooker's which they allege is against his mind and judgment.

Mr. Sims. I would ask for Mrs. Hutchinson to remember that the humble will teach—I have said that before and therefore I will leave the place with her and do consider of many expressions that she hath spoken to her husband, but I will not enlarge myself.

Mr. Endicot. Considering that which has already been said, I would like to have a word or two. I have heard of many revelations of Mr. Hutchinson's but they were reports, but Mrs. Hutchinson, I see, does maintain some by this discourse and I think that it is a special providence of God to hear what she has said. Now there is a revelation, you see, which she does expect as a miracle. She says she now suffers, and, let us do what we will, she shall be delivered by a miracle. I hope the court takes notice of the vanity of her statements and heat of her spirit. Now because her reverend teacher is here I should desire that he would speak freely whether he condescends to such speeches or revelations as have been here spoken of, and he will give a great deal of content.

Mr. Cotton. As you wish, Sir. There are two sorts of revelations, there are *[the original text is here missing]* or against the word besides scripture both which *[the original text is here missing]* [fan]tastical and tending to danger more ways than one—there is another sort which the apostles pray that the believing Ephesians may partake in *[Eph. 1.17]*, and those are such as are breathed by the spirit of God and are never dispensed but in a word of God and according to a word of God.

And though the word of revelation be rare in common speech and we make it uncouth in our ordinary expressions, yet notwithstanding, being understood in the scripture sense, I think they are not only lawful but such as Christians may receive and God bear witness to it in his word, and usually he expresses it in the ministry of the word and accompanies it by his spirit, or else it is in the reading of the word in some chapter or verse and whenever it comes it comes flying upon the wings of the spirit.

Mr. Endicot. You satisfy me and therefore I desire to give your judgment of Mrs. Hutchinson; you have heard what she has said and all the circumstances thereof.

Mr. Cotton. I ask whether by a miracle she means a work above nature or by some wonderful providence *[a normal event, but directed by God for a specific goal]*, for that is called a miracle often in the psalms.

Mrs. H. I desire to speak to our teacher. You know Sir, what he *[Daniel]* declares, though he does not know himself *[text missing]* now either of these ways or at this present time it shall be done, yet I would not have the court so to understand me that he will deliver me now even at this present time.

Dep. Gov. I desire Mr. Cotton to tell us whether you approve of Mrs. Hutchinson's revelations as she lays them down.

Mr. Cotton. I do not know whether I do understand her, but this I say, if she expects a deliverance in a way of providence—then I cannot deny it.

Dep. Gov. No Sir we are not asking that.

Mr. Cotton. If it were by way of a miracle then I would suspect it.

Dep. Gov. Do you think that her revelations are true?

Mr. Cotton. That she might have some special providence of God to help her is a thing that I cannot bear witness against.

Dep. Gov. Good Sir, I ask whether this revelation be of God or no?

Mr. Cotton. I should desire to know whether the sentence of the court will bring her to any calamity, and then I should know of her whether she expects to be delivered from that calamity by a miracle or a providence of God.

Mrs. H. When I said by a providence of God, I meant that I expect to be delivered from some calamity that will come to me.

Gov. The case is then different and will not stand with us now, but I see a marvelous providence of God to bring things to this pass that they are. We have been hearkening about the trial of this thing, and now the mercy of God by a providence answered our desires and made her lay open her self and the ground of all these disturbances to be by revelations, for we receive no such *[the original text is here missing]* made out of the ministry of the word *[the original text is here missing]* and so one scripture after another. But meanwhile, there is no use of the ministry of the word nor of any clear call of God by his word. But the ground work of her revelations is the immediate revelation of the spirit and not by the ministry of the word.

And that is the means by which she has very much abused the country. She has taught them that they shall look for revelations and are not bound to the ministry of the word, but God will teach them by immediate revelations. This has been the ground of all these tumults and troubles, and I would that those people were all cut off from us that trouble us, for this is the thing that hath been the root of all the mischief.

Court. We all consent with you.

Gov. Yes, it is the most desperate enthusiasm in the world, because nothing but a word of scripture comes to her mind and then an interpretation is made [which Hutchinson thinks is inspired by the Holy Spirit] which is not even relevant to the subject, and this is her revelation. But it is impossible for the word of scripture and the Holy Spirit not to mean the same thing.

Mr. Endicot. I speak in reference to Mr. Cotton. I am tender of you, Sir, and there lies much upon you in this particular circumstance. For the answer of Mr. Cotton does not free him from the suspicion that his last answer brought upon him. Therefore I beseech you that you'd be pleased to speak a word regarding what Mrs. Hutchinson has spoken of her revelations, as you have heard the manner of it. Whether do you support her or not.

Mr. Cotton. I will repeat myself, Sir, and my answer is plain: if she looks for deliverance from the hand of God by his providence, and the revelations are in a word of scripture or according to a word, that I cannot deny.

Mr. Endicot. You give me satisfaction.

Dep. Gov. No, no, he gives me none at all.

Mr. Cotton. But if it is in the form of a miracle or a revelation without the word, that I do not assent to, but look at it as a delusion, and I think she does also, as I understand her.

Dep. Gov. Sir, you weary me and do not satisfy me.

Mr. Cotton. Please Sir, give me an opportunity to express myself. In that sense she speaks I dare not bear witness against it.

Mr. Nowell. I think that it is devilish delusion.

Gov. Of all the revelations that ever I read of, I never read any similar ground laid as for this. The Enthusiasts and Anabaptists had never the like.

Mr. Cotton. You know Sir that their revelations broach new matters of faith and doctrine.

Gov. These do as well, and if they are let alone, they will multiply. I do acknowledge that there are such revelations as do concur with the word *[of the Bible]* but there has not been any of this nature.

The Trial of Anne Hutchinson

Dep. Gov. I never saw revelations like these among the Anabaptists, therefore I am sorry that Mr. Cotton should stand to justify her.

Mr. Peters. I can say the same and this could be called enthusiasm, and I think what our Brother Cotton spoke about is very debatable *[text missing]* an immediate promise that he will deliver them *[text missing]* in a day of trouble.

Gov. It overthrows all.

Dep Gov. These disturbances that have come among the Germans have all been based on revelations, and so those that have vented them have stirred up their hearers to take up arms against their prince and to cut the throats one of another, and these have been the fruits of them, and whether the devil may inspire the same into their hearts here, I do not know, for I am fully persuaded that Mrs. Hutchinson is deluded by the devil because the spirit of God speaks truth in all his servants.

Gov. I am persuaded that the revelation that she brings forth is a delusion.

All the court except for two or three ministers cry out: we all believe it we all believe it.

Mr. Endicot. I suppose that the whole world can see where the foundations of these troubles lie.

Mr. Eliot. I say there is an expectation of things promised, but to have a particular revelation of things that will fall out, there is no such thing in the scripture.

Gov. We will not limit the word of God.

Mr. Collicut. It is a great burden to us that he should justify these revelations. I would entreat him to answer concerning the statement about the destruction of England.

Gov. Mr. Cotton is not called to answer to any thing, but we are to deal with the party here standing before us.

Mr. Bartholomew. My wife has said that Mr. Wheelwright was not acquainted with this way until she imparted it unto him.

Mr. Brown. In as much as I am called to speak, I would therefore speak the mind of our brethren. Though we had sufficient grounds for the censure before, yet now that she has vented herself and I find such flat contradiction to the scripture in what she says, as to that in the first to the Hebrews—God at sundry times spake to our fathers.[15] For my part I understand that scripture and other scripture of the Lord Jesus Christ, and the apostle writing to Timothy said that the scripture is able to make one perfect—therefore I say the mind of the brethren—I think she deserves no less a censure than hath been already past but rather something more, for this is the foundation of all mischief and of all those bastardly things which have that great meeting has been causing. They have all come from this cursed fountain.

Gov. Seeing the court has thus declared itself and having heard the charges laid against Mrs. Hutchinson and especially what she by the providence of God hath declared freely without being asked, if therefore it be the mind of the court, looking at her as the principal cause of all our trouble, that they would now consider what is to be done to her.

Mr. Coddington. There is one thing objected against the meetings. What if she designed to edify her own family in her own meetings privately with no other guests?

---

[15] Hebrews 1.1,2, "God, who at sundry times and in divers manners spake in time past unto the fathers by the prophets, Hath in these last days spoken unto us by his Son, whom he hath appointed heir of all things, by whom also he made the worlds." The point is that there was a need for prophets before Christ came; now there is none.

Gov. If you have nothing else to say but that, it is a pity Mr. Coddington that you interrupt us in proceeding to censure.

Mr. Coddington. I would say more Sir, another thing you lay to her charge is her speech to the elders. I do not see any clear witness against her, and you know it is a rule of the court that a man may not be judge and an accuser too. I do not speak to disparage our elders and their callings, but I do not see any thing that they accuse her of witnessed against her, and therefore I do not see how she should be censured for that. And for the other thing which she spoke occasionally by the spirit of God, you know the spirit of God witnesses with our spirits, and there is no truth in scripture but God bears witness to it by his spirit, therefore I would entreat you to consider whether those things you have alleged against her deserve such a censure as you are about to pass, whether it is banishment or imprisonment. And again here is nothing proved about the elders, only that she said they did not teach a covenant of grace so clearly as Mr. Cotton did and that they were in the state of the apostles before the ascension. Why I hope this may not be offensive nor any wrong to them.

Gov. Even if you disregard all that was spoken with the ministers, her own speeches here have been ground enough for us to proceed upon.

Mr. Coddington. I beseech you not to speak to force things along, for I do not see any justice in the court in all your proceedings. Here is no law of God that she has broken nor any law of the country that she has broken, and therefore she deserves no censure, and if she say that the elders preach as the apostles did, why they preached a covenant of grace and what wrong is that to them, for it is without question that the apostles did preach a covenant of grace, though not with that power, till they received the manifestation of the spirit, therefore I pray consider what you do, for here is no law of God or man broken.

Mr. Harlakenden. Things thus spoken will stick. I would therefore that the assembly take notice that here is none that condemns the meeting of Christian women; but in such a way and for such an end that it is to be detested. And even if the matter of the elders be taken away, yet there is enough besides to condemn her, but I shall speak no further.

Dep. Gov. We shall be all sick with fasting.

Mr. Colburn. I dissent from the censure of banishment.

Mr. Stoughton. The censure which the court is about to pass in my conscience is as much as she deserves, but because she desires witness and there is none in way of witness, therefore I shall desire that no offence be taken if I do not formally condemn her because she hath not been formally convicted as others are by witness upon oath.

Mr. Coddington. This is a scruple to me also, because Solomon said, every man is partial in his own cause and here is none that accuses her but the elders, and she spoke nothing to them but in private, and I do not know what rule they had to make the thing publick. Secret things ought to be spoken in secret and publick things in publick, therefore I think they have broken the rules of God's word.[16]

Gov. What was spoken in the presence of many is not to be made secret.

Mr. Coddington. But that was spoken but to a few and in private.

Gov. Because Mr. Stoughton is not satisfied, to the end all scruples may be removed we will desire the elders to take their oaths.

Here now was a great whispering among the ministers, some drew back others were animated on.

---

[16] Proverbs 25.9, "Debate thy matter with thy neighbor, and discover not the secret to another."

The Trial of Anne Hutchinson

Mr. Eliot. If the court calls us out to swear we will swear.

Gov. Any two of you will serve.

Mr. Stoughton. There are two things that I would look to discharge my conscience of, first to hear what they testify upon oath and secondly to—

Gov. It is required of you, Mr. Weld, and Mr. Eliot.

Mr. Weld and Mr. Eliot. We will be willing.

Gov. We'll give them their oaths. You shall swear to the truth and nothing but the truth as far as you know. So help you God. What do you remember of her..

Mr. Eliot. I do remember and I have it written that which she spoke first was, the fear of man is a snare, why should she be afraid but would speak freely. The question being asked whether there was a difference between Mr. Cotton and us she said there was a broad difference. I would not stick upon words. The thing she said was that Mr.Cotton did preach a covenant of grace and we of works and she gave this reason---to put a work *[of holiness]* in point of evidence *[of salvation]* is a revealing upon a work. We did labour then to convince her that our doctrine was the same with Mr. Cotton's. She said no, for we were not sealed. That is all I shall say.

Gov. What say you, Mr. Weld?

Mr. Weld. I will speak to the things themselves—these two things I am fully clear in— she did make a difference in three things, the first I was not so clear in, but that she said that we were not able ministers of the new testament and that we were not clear in our experience because we were not sealed.

Mr. Eliot. I do further remember this also, that she said we were not able ministers of the gospel because we were but like the apostles before the ascension.

Mr. Coddington. This was I hope no disparagement to you.

Gov. Well, we see in the court that she continually says and unsays things.

Mr. Peters. I was much grieved that she should say that our ministry was legal. Upon which, we had a meeting as you know and this was the same. She told us that there was a broad difference between Mr. Cotton and us. Now if Mr. Cotton do hold forth things more clearly than we, it was our grief we did not hold it so clearly as he did, and upon those grounds that you have heard.

Mr. Coddington. I don't think that there was wrong in saying that you were not able ministers of the new testament or that you were like the apostles—methinks the comparison is very good.

Gov. Well, you remember that she said just now that she should be delivered from this calamity.

Mr. Cotton. I remember she said she should be delivered by God's providence, whether now or at another time she knew not.

Mr. Peters. I profess I thought Mr. Cotton would never have sided with her.

Mr. Stoughton. I say now this testimony doth convince me in the thing, and I am fully satisfied the words were pernicious, and the frame of her spirit holds forth the same.

Gov. The court hath already declared themselves satisfied concerning the things you hear, and concerning the troublesomeness of her spirit and the danger of her course amongst us, which is not to be suffered. Therefore if it be the mind of the court that Mrs. Hutchinson for these things that appear before us is unfit for our society and if it be the mind of the court that she shall be banished out of our liberties and imprisoned till she be sent away, let them hold up their hands. *[All but three raise hands]* All but three. Those that are contrary minded hold up yours *[Mr. Coddington and Mr. Colborn, only]*.

Mr. Jennison. I cannot hold up my hand one way or the other, I will explain myself if the court require it.

Gov. Mrs. Hutchinson, the sentence of the court you hear is that you are banished from out of our jurisdiction as being a woman not fit for our society, and are to be imprisoned till the court shall send you away.

Mrs. H. I desire to know wherefore I am banished?

Gov. Say no more, the court knows wherefore and is satisfied.

JOHN WINTHROP: "A MODEL OF CHRISTIAN CHARITY"

[You can find the full text of this sermon at the Web site for the Hanover Historical Texts Project, <http://history.hanover.edu/texts/winthmod.html>.]

"A Model of Christian Charity": by Winthrop, delivered to the puritans aboard the *Arbella*, June 1630.

God Almighty, in His most holy and wise providence, has so disposed of the condition of mankind, as in all times some must be rich; some poor; some high and eminent in power and dignity; others mean and in subjection.

The Reason Hereof: first, to hold conformity with the rest of His works, being delighted to show forth the glory of His wisdom in the variety and difference of the creatures and the glory of His power, in ordering all these differences for the preservation and good of the whole; and the glory of His greatness in that, as it is the glory of princes to have many officers, so this Great King will have many stewards, counting Himself more honored in dispensing His gifts to man by man than if He did it by His own immediate hand. Second, that he might have the more occasion to manifest the work of His spirit; first, upon the wicked in moderating and restraining them, so that the rich and mighty should not eat up the poor, nor the poor and despised rise up against their superiors and shake off their yoke; second, in the regenerate in exercising His graces in them, as in the great ones their love, mercy, gentleness, etc.; in the poor and inferior sort, their faith, patience, obedience.

Third, that every man might have need of others, and from hence they might be all knit more nearly together in the bond of brotherly affection. . . .

There are two rules whereby we are to walk one toward another: *justice and mercy*. These are always distinguished in their act and in their object . . . There is likewise a double law by which we are regulated in our conversation one toward another: in both the former respects, the law of nature and the law of grace . . . By the first of these laws, man . . . is commanded to love his neighbor as himself . . . The law of grace has some difference from the former as in these respects: First, the law of nature was given to man in the estate of innocence [prior to Adam and Eve's fall]; the law of grace in the estate of regeneracy. The law of gospel propounds a difference of seasons and occasions. There is a time when a Christian must sell all and give to the poor as they did in the apostles' times. There is a time also when Christians (though they give not all yet) must give beyond their ability . . . Likewise, community of perils calls for extraordinary liberality and so does community in some special service for the church. Lastly, when there is no other means whereby our Christian brother may be relieved in this distress, we must help him beyond our ability, rather than tempt God in putting him upon help by miraculous or extraordinary means. This duty of mercy is exercised in giving, lending, and forgiving.

Question: What rule must we observe in lending?

Answer: You must observe whether your brother has present or probable or possible means of repaying you, or if none of these, you must give to him according to his necessity, rather than lend to him as he asks . . . if his means of repaying you are only probable or possible, then he is an object of mercy and you must lend to him though there is danger of losing it. Deut. 15:7: "If any of thy brethren be poor . . . thou shalt lend him sufficient."

Question: What rule must we observe in forgiving?

Answer: Whether you lend by way of commerce or in mercy. If he has nothing to repay, you must forgive him. In all these and like cases Christ gave a general rule in Matthew 7:22: "Whatsoever you would that men should do to you, do ye the same to them also."

Question: What rule must we observe and walk by in the case of a community of peril?

Answer: The same as before, but with more enlargement toward others and less respect toward ourselves and our own right. Hence, in the primitive church they sold all and had all things in common, nor did any man say that what he possessed was his own. Herein are four principles to be expounded:

First, we are a company professing ourselves fellow members of Christ . . . Though we are absent from each other by many miles, and have our employments at far distance, we ought to account ourselves knitted together by this bond of love, and live in the exercise of it. . . .

Second, the work we have in hand is by mutual consent with a special overruling Providence, with a more than ordinary mandate from the churches of Christ to seek out a place to live and associate under a due form of government both civil and ecclesiastical. In such cases as this the care of the public must hold sway over all private interests. Third, our end is to improve our lives to do more service to the Lord and to comfort and increase the body of Christ of which we are members, so that ourselves and our posterity may be better preserved from the common corruptions of this evil world in order to serve the Lord and work out our salvation under the power and purity of His holy ordinances. Fourth, the means whereby this must be effected are twofold. First, we must not content ourselves with ordinary means . . . That which most people in their churches only profess as a truth, we must bring into familiar and constant practice . . . When God gives a special commission He wants it strictly observed in every article . . . Thus stands the case between God and us. We are entered into covenant with Him for this work. We have taken out a commission. The Lord has given us leave to draw our own articles; we have promised to base our actions on these ends, and we have asked Him for favor and blessing. Now if the Lord shall please to hear us, and bring us in peace to the place we desire, then He has ratified this covenant and sealed our commission, and will expect strict performance of the articles contained in it. But if we neglect to observe these articles, which are the ends we have propounded, and—dissembling with our God—shall embrace this present world and prosecute our carnal intentions, the Lord will surely break out in wrath against us and be revenged of such a perjured people, and He will make us know the price of a breach of such a covenant.

We shall keep the unity of the spirit in the bond of peace. The Lord will command a blessing on us in all our ways, so that we shall see much more of His wisdom, power, goodness and truth than we have formerly known. We shall find that the God of Israel is among us, and ten of us shall be able to resist a thousand of our enemies. The Lord will make our name a praise and glory, so that men shall say of succeeding plantations: "The Lord make it like that of New England." For we must consider that we shall be like a City upon a Hill; the eyes of all people are on us.

If we deal falsely with our God in this work we have undertaken and so cause Him to withdraw His present help from us, we shall be made a story and a byword throughout the world; we shall open the mouths of enemies to speak evil of the ways of God and all believers in God; we shall shame the faces of many of God's worthy servants and cause their prayers to be turned into curses upon us, till we are forced out of the new land where we are going.

JOHN WINTHROP ON LIBERTY (1645)

[The following is an excerpt from a speech Winthrop made to the General Court. It is taken from his many-times-reprinted Journal. The speech has been slightly modernized and abridged.]

There is a twofold liberty, natural (I mean as our nature is now corrupt [because all people are sinners]) and civil or federal. The first is common to man with beasts and other creatures. By this, man, as he stands in relation to man simply, hath liberty to do what he wishes to do; it is a liberty to evil as well as to good. This liberty is incompatible and inconsistent with authority and cannot endure the least restraint of the most just authority. The exercise and maintaining of this liberty makes men grow more evil and in time to be worse than brute beasts . . . This [kind of liberty] is that great enemy of truth and peace, that wild beast, which all of the ordinances of God are bent against, to restrain and subdue it.

The other kind of liberty I call civil or federal; it may also be termed moral, in reference to the covenant between God and man, in the moral law, and the politic covenants and constitutions amongst men themselves. This liberty is the proper end and object of authority and cannot subsist without it; and it is a liberty to that only which is good, just, and honest. This liberty you are to stand for, with the hazard (not only of your goods, but) of your lives, if need be. Whatsoever opposes this is not authority but a distemper thereof.

This liberty is maintained and exercised in a way of subjection to authority; it is of the same kind of liberty wherewith Christ hath made us free. The woman's own choice makes such a man her husband; yet, being so chosen, he is her lord, and she is to be subject to him, yet in a way of liberty, not of bondage; and a true wife accounts her subjection her honor and freedom. . . .

Such is the liberty of the church under the authority of Christ, her king and husband; his yoke is so easy and sweet to her as a bride's ornaments. . . .

Even so, brethren, it will be between you and your magistrates. If you want to stand for your natural corrupt liberties, and will do what is good in your own eyes, you will not endure the least weight of authority, but will murmur, and oppose, and be always striving to shake off that yoke; but if you will be satisfied to enjoy such civil and lawful liberties, such as Christ allows you, then will you quietly and cheerfully submit unto that authority which is set over you, in all the administrations of it, for your good. Wherein, if we fail at any time, we hope we shall be willing (by God's assistance) to hearken to good advice from any of you, or in any other way of God; so shall your liberties be preserved in upholding the honor and power of authority amongst you.

JOHN WINTHROP AND HENRY VANE DEBATE THE IMMIGRATION ORDER (1637)

[The immigration order, passed in the May 1637, General Court, allowed no immigrants to stay in the colony for more than three weeks without the permission of the magistrates. Any town that subsequently sold or gave any immigrant who had been denied residency land or any people that housed them were subject to heavy fines. Winthrop wrote a defense of the order and Vane wrote a reply. Excerpts from Winthrop's defense, in italics, and Vane's response are printed below.[17] They are taken from The Hutchinson Papers (Albany, NY, 1865), 84-96. The excerpts have been abridged and archaic word usage has been changed. Winthrop argues that Wheelwright's opinions are dangerous to the commonwealth and that the commonwealth has a right to keep out people that would endanger it. Vane objects that the problem with the order is that it has no guidelines for the magistrates and so gives them a dangerous amount of uncontrolled power. Arbitrary power unguided by divine rules, Vane warns, is typical of the spirit of the Catholic Church. Moreover, the gospel, such as Wheelwright preaches, cannot be kept out of a Christian colony. Massachusetts is not semi-independent, as Winthrop seems to think. This arbitrary order deprives the king of his rights and his subjects of their liberties.]

Winthrop: No commonwealth can be founded but by free consent. The persons so incorporating have a public and relative interest each in other, and in the place of their cohabitation and goods, and laws &c. and in all the means of their welfare, so as none other can claim privilege with them but by free consent.

Vane: At best [this] is a description of a commonwealth at large and not of such a commonwealth as this (as is said) which is not only Christian, but dependent upon the grant also of our Sovereign. Now if you will define a Christian commonwealth there must be put in such a consent as is according to God, a subjecting to such a government as is according to Christ. And if you will define a corporation incorporated by virtue of the grant of our Sovereign, it must be such a consent as the grant requires and permits. Our commonwealth, we fear, would be twice miserable if Christ and the King should be shut out.

Winthrop: If we here be a corporation established by free consent, if the place of our cohabitation be our own, then no man has right to come into us &c without our consent.

Vane: Our consent, regulated by the word [of the Bible] and suitable to our patent ought to be required, not this vast and boundless consent here spoken of. The question is [not

---

[17] Hutchinson was the first to publish the documents in their entirety and the first to attribute the reply to Vane. An excerpt had been published in the 17th century that attributed the reply to Wheelwright, but in a further response, not reproduced here, Winthrop identifies his opponent as a member of the General Court when the law was passed who supports Wheelwright, which agrees with Hutchison.

whether the commonwealth can reject people] but whether persons may be rejected or admitted [only] upon the unbounded consent or dissent of magistrates. Men are not to keep off whatever appears to tend to their ruin, but what really does so. It appeared to the chief priests and pharisees that if our blessed Saviour were let alone, it would tend to their ruin, John 11. 47, 48, and therefore used means to keep it off by rejecting Christ and his gospel, and yet we hope you will not say they were bound to do so. It appears to the Natives here (who by your definition are complete commonwealths among themselves) that the cohabitation of the English with them tends to their utter ruin, yet we believe you will not say they may lawfully keep us out upon that ground, for our cohabitation with them may tend to their conversion and so to their eternal salvation.

Winthrop: To deny a man that which he has no right unto, is neither sin nor injury.

Vane: We may not deny residence to any of his majesty's subjects without just grounds, except we will do injury both to the King and his subjects, who have adventured both their estates and lives [by crossing the Atlantic] to enjoy those privileges and liberties which he has granted them. The law does not only prohibit those whom the magistrates shall dislike to plant in those places uninhabited, though in an orderly maner, but to make their abode in friends' houses, either given or sold, or rented, which are lawful means of obtaining right. Now if the king's majesty give me right, if this state at their pleasure take this away and expell men from the same, what were this but to exercise robbery, and to vex the poor and the needy, and oppress the stranger wrongfully, a sin forerunning desolation, Ezek. 22. 29, and such a one as will more ruin the state the execution thereof than those persons (whom the law intend to expel) were the law abolished.

Winthrop: A family is a little commonwealth and a commonwealth is a great family. Now as a family is not bound to entertain all comers, no more is a commonwealth.

Vane: A master of a family has another kind of right to his house and estate than this commonwealth has to all the houses and lands within this patent. The master of a family may bequeath his whole estate to his wife and children, and so may not the body of this commonwealth to theirs. The king will look for some right, nor may we blame him if he do. Many are no members of this commonwealth [because they are not freemen], and yet have good right both to houses and lands here. Many members of this state agree not to this law, but have protested against it as sinful and unwholesome, and yet we hope have as good right to their houses, goods, and lands as the master of the family has to his. It is to be feared that such pleas of right [as Winthrop is claiming] will work more trouble to this state if they be noised abroad than the entertainment of those people against whom this law is made.

Winthrop: It is a general rule, it is worse to receive a man whom we must cast out than to deny him admittance.

Vane: Perhaps this may show the Court's intent, for this intimation we have from hence: that the intent of the commonwealth is to cast out all such as have been received in times past who are of the same judgment with them whom the magistrates will not admit but cast out, though with a great deal more dishonesty [i.e., Winthrop and his allies are intending to expel the supporters of Wheelwright].

The Trial of Anne Hutchinson

Winthrop: The rule of the Apostle, John 2.10. is, that such as come and bring not the true doctrine with them should not be received to house, and by the same reason not into the commonwealth.

Vane: If the order now in question were but conformable to this rule of the Apostle, none would oppose it, but the order sets down no rule for the magistrates to walk by in that admittance or rejection of such as come, but leaves it to their boundless consent or dissent. Nay, such were the expressions of the same, in the court, who had a hand in this law, as clears it to us that this law opposes directly this rule. For such as do bring the doctrine intended in the text are the persons which are aimed at to be denied residence, as sad experience also in the execution has given us in part to see already, and we fear in the future will yet do more.

Winthrop: Whereas it is said that this law was made of purpose to keep away such as are of Mr. Wheelwright's judgment (admit it were so which yet I cannot confess) where is the evil of it? It we conceive and find by sad experience that his opinions are such, as by his own profession cannot stand with external peace, may we not provide for our peace by keeping of such as would strengthen him and infect others with such dangerous opinions such as will cause divisions and make people look at their magistrates, ministers, and brethren as enemies to Christ and Antichrists?

Vane: You find fault with his opinions because he said they could not stand with external peace. He affirmed indeed that the preaching of the gospel could not stand with external peace, and does not the word of God hold this forth? Our Saviour came not to send peace but a sword, Matth. 10. 34. When news of Christ come, Herod and all Jerusalem is troubled, Matth. 2.3. In the second place you object to his opinions because they make divisions. The gospel which he or any man holds forth will cause divisions as a side effect, Matth. 10. 34, 35. If he be blamed for this, Christ cannot be excused. The third thing you allege is that his opinions make people look at their magistrates, ministers, and brethren as antichristian, enemies to Christ, but we know no such doctrine which he taught. All he delivered concerning this matter was a description of the way of works and antichristianism, and so far as magistrates and ministers walk in that way, they are to be looked at as antichristian.

This law we judge to be most wicked and sinful, and that for these reasons.
Because this law does leave these weighty matters of the commonwealth of receiving or rejecting such as come over to the approval of magistrates, and rests these things upon the judgment of man, whereas the judgment is God's, Deut. 1.17. This is made a ground work of gross popery. That law which gives that without limitations to man, which is proper to God, cannot be just.

Because here is liberty given by this law to expel and reject those which are most eminent Christians, if they suit not with the disposition of the magistrates.
This law will not give unto the King's majesty his right of planting some of his subjects among us, unless they please the magistrates. Christ bids us not to forget to entertain strangers, Heb. 13.2. But here by this law we must not entertain for any continuance of time such strangers as the magistrates like not, though they be never so gracious, unless we will forfeit unto them our whole estates [by fines]. Many other laws there are of Christ which this law dashes against, and therefore is most wicked and sinful.

JOHN WINTHROP'S CONVERSION NARRATIVE (1637)

[Winthrop wrote this account of his search for assurance of salvation at the beginning of 1637, around the time of Wheelwright's fast day sermon. He probably circulated it. It is a classic, psychologically astute account of a puritan's conversion. It also gives some sense of Winthrop's character. Winthrop was from an upper-class third-generation puritan family. By today's standards he would plainly be considered a religious child. Yet by his standards, he did not get converted until he was almost an adult. In addition, this narrative is an important example of Winthrop's efforts to lower the heat of controversy in Massachusetts. In his account of his own spiritual struggles, Winthrop is showing that both sides in Massachusetts are making valid points, even though the orthodox ministers are, overall, the most reliable guides to salvation.

When Winthrop was first converted as a teenager, he was full of enthusiasm and did not doubt his salvation. As his enthusiasm wore off, so did his conviction that he had been saved. To get that conviction back, he carefully examined his holiness (sanctification) and struggled hard to act as pious as he could. He got some comfort through this approach, but every time he sinned, he lost his assurance of his salvation. His struggles and doubts led him to examine both the covenant of grace and his own heart more carefully. As a result, he had a mystical experience of God's love to him, such as Anne Hutchinson glorified. This experience gave him a sense of assurance of salvation so intense that he never entirely lost it again.

Cotton and Hutchinson could have been convinced of the genuineness of Winthrop's ultimate experience of assurance, because it came NOT from his good works (i.e., "I've sure been good today at refraining from sin") but from the immediate seal, or witness of the Spirit: from God's gift of grace (i.e., "I can sense God's infinite love for me, which makes me long all the more to behave in a way that justifies HIS justification of me"). BUT Winthrop's assurance only comes a decade after his initial assurance, which was through sanctification. And Hutchinson denies that first assurance can first come through sanctification. Indeed, she denies that sanctification can ever generate assurance.

Moreover, Winthrop regards doubting and unsteady assurance as an important part of his spiritual development. It drove him to look ever more carefully at himself. And even if he did not fundamentally question his salvation anymore, he continued to be distressed by the imperfection of his holiness.

Thus, Anne Hutchinson is right to say that it is ultimately best to look to a mystical experience of Christ for assurance of salvation and not to your own struggles. Winthrop himself has experienced the immediate witness of the Spirit that she praises so highly. Where she is wrong is that ordinary Christians first have to go through a long process of struggling with their sins and repeatedly gaining and then losing their sense of assurance of salvation before they can genuinely enjoy the kind of experience that she advocates. This long, painful process is the only way that they can get to know both themselves and the nature of the covenant of grace that saves them. If you dismiss the validity of this process of doubt and struggle, as Hutchinson seems to do, you will probably only fool yourself about the state of your soul. Winthrop also makes it plain that respect for ministers is a fundamental sign of true holiness.

Winthrop at the end of his account in effect thanks opponents like Hutchinson for making their point. Winthrop has spiritually benefited from what they have to say. But they need to stop being so one-sided. They should realize that they need to learn from the people they are attacking so fiercely. If they don't realize that, he will do his best to drive them out of the colony.

Note the third paragraph from the end and realize that Winthrop is certainly talking at least in part about the strains of planning and starting the colony and about what kept him going in these stressful times.

Winthrop's account can be found in Robert C. Winthrop, Life and Letters of John Winthrop, *2 vols., 2d ed. (Boston, 1869), 2:165-74, and in a slightly different version from another manuscript in the* Winthrop Papers, *Allyn B. Forbe et al., 5 vols (Boston, 1929-47), 3:338-44. The version below has been freely modified for purposes of clarity.]*

JOHN WINTHROP'S ACCOUNT OF HIS RELIGIOUS EXPERIENCE

When I was a child I was inclined to all kind of wickedness (so far as my youth allowed me), although my religious education prevented me from being tempted to swear and scorn religion. When I was ten, in some great fright or danger, I prayed unto God, and found an answer. The memory of that for many years made me think that God loved me, but it did not make me any better.

After I was 12 years old, I began to become more religious. I thought I had more understanding in theology than many my age; for when I read some good books I conceived that I already understood many of the ideas, although I did not know how I should come by such knowledge (but I later realized that it was by logical deduction). Yet I was still very wild, and dissolute, and as years came on my lusts grew stronger. They were still restrained by my natural reason however, whereby I had the command of myself to do whatever I wished. I would as occasion required write frivolous letters, but if the situation called for it I could write others of wise and godly advice.

When I was about 14, at Cambridge, I fell into a lingering fever, which took away the comfort of my life. Because I was neglected, and despised there, I went up and down mourning with my self. Being deprived of my youthful joys, I turned to God, whom I believed to be very good and merciful, and would welcome any that would come to him, especially such a young soul, and so well qualified as I took myself to be; so as I took pleasure in drawing near to him.

But how my heart was disturbed by my sins, or what thoughts I had of Christ I do not remember. But I was willing to love God, and therefore I thought He loved me. But as soon as I recovered my perfect health, and found other things to take pleasure in, I forgot my former acquaintance with God, and fell to former lusts, and grew worse then before. Yet some good moods I had now and then, and restraint through my natural Conscience, by which the Lord preserved me from some foul sins [*given Winthrop's age, this is probably a reference to sexual temptations*]. But my lusts were so masterly as no good could fasten upon me, otherwise than to hold me to ordinary religious duties, for I cared for nothing but how to satisfy my voluptuous heart.

When I was about 18 years old, (and my parents considering me a man in appearance and understanding) I married into a family in the parish of Mr. Culverwell in Essex [*a famous puritan preacher*]. Listening to him was the first time that I found preaching to come to my heart with power (for before I found only light to my understanding). After that I found the same in the ministry of many others. There began to be some change which I perceived in myself, and which others took notice of. Now I began to come under strong exercises of Conscience: (yet by fits only). I could no longer dally with Religion. God put my soul to sad tasks sometimes, which the flesh would shake off, and outwear still. The merciful Lord would not thus be answered, but notwithstanding all my stubbornness and unkind rejections of mercy, He did not leave me till He had overcome my heart to give up itself to him, and to bid farewell to all the world, and until my heart could answer, Lord what wilt thou have me to doe? [*Acts 9:6*]

Now I came to some peace and comfort in God and in his ways, I loved a Christian, and the very ground he went upon. I honored a faithful minister in my heart and could have kissed his feet: Now I grew full of zeal (which outran my knowledge and carried me sometimes beyond my Calling) and was very liberal to any good work. I had an unsatiable thirst after the word of God and could not miss a good sermon, though many miles off, especially from preachers who probed deep into the conscience. I had also a great desire to draw others to God. It pitied my heart to see men pay so little attention to their souls, and to despise that happiness which I knew to be better than all the world besides. My success in my endeavors gave me much encouragement. But those feelings were not constant but very unsettled.

I developed a reputation for piety (which did not a little puff me up). People would come to me for advice, and if I heard of any that were in trouble of mind I usually went to comfort them. I gave myself up to the study of Divinity, and intended to enter into the ministry if my friends had not diverted me.

But as my reputation grew, I grew also in pride of my gifts, and under temptations which set me to look to my evidence that I had been saved more carefully than I had done before (for the great change which God had wrought in me, and the general approval of good ministers and other Christians, kept me from making any great question of my good Estate). Yet my secret Corruptions and some tremblings of heart (which was greatest when I was among the most Godly persons) put me to some plunges; but especially when I perceived a great decay in my zeal and love, etc. I heard of a better assurance by the seal [*or immediate witness*] of the spirit, which I also knew by the word of God, but I could not nor dared not say that ever I had it.

Finding by reading of Mr. Perkins and other books that a damned person might (in appearance) attain to as much piety as I had done; and finding much hollowness and vainglory in my heart, I began to grow very sad, and did not know what to doe. I was ashamed to ask for advice from any minister that knew me; I feared it would shame my self and religion also that such an eminent professor as I was accounted should discover such Corruptions as I found in myself, and had in all this time attained no better evidence of salvation. I feared I would prove to be a hypocrite. It was too late to begin anew: I would never truly repent, since I had already repented so often. It was like Hell to me to think of that in Hebr. 6 [*"It is impossible for those who were once enlightened . . . if they shall fall away, to renew them again unto repentance"*].

Yet sometimes I asked carefully worded questions to the most Godly ministers as I met, which gave me ease for the present. But my heart could find nowhere to rest. I grew very sad and melancholy; and now to hear others applaud me was a dart through my liver. I feared I was not sound at the root. Sometimes I had thoughts of breaking from my profession, and to proclaim myself a Hypocrite. But those troubles came not all at once but by fits, for sometimes I should find refreshing in prayer, and sometimes in the Love that I had to the saints: which though it were but poor comfort (for I did not dare say before God that I loved them in truth) yet the Lord upheld me, and many times outward occasions put these fears out of my thoughts.

Upon these and the like troubles, when I could by no means attain sure and settled peace; and that which I did get was still broken off upon every infirmity; I concluded there was no way to help it, but by walking more close with God and more strict observation of all duties. Hereby though I put my self to many a needless task, and deprived my self of many lawful Comforts, yet my peace would fail upon every small occasion, and I was held long under great bondage to the Law (sin, and humble my self; and sin, and to humiliation again; and so day after day) yet neither got strength to my sanctification nor bettered my Evidence, but was brought to such bondage, as I dared not to use any recreation, nor meddle with any worldly business, etc. for fear of breaking my peace (which even such as it was, was very precious to me). But this would not hold neither for then I grew very melancholy and my thoughts wearied me and wasted my spirits.

Being in this Condition it pleased the Lord to manifest unto me the difference between the Covenant of Grace, and the Covenant of works. This Covenant of Grace began to take great impression in me and I thought I had now enough. To have Christ freely, and to be justified freely was very sweet to me; and upon sound warrant (as I conceived) but I would not say with any confidence, it had been sealed to me, but I rather took occasion to bee more remiss in my spiritual watch, and so more loose in my Conversation.

I was now about 30 years of age, and now was the time come that the Lord would reveal Christ unto me whom I had long desired, but not so earnestly as since I came to see more clearly into the Covenant of free grace. First therefore hee laid a sore affliction upon me wherein he laid me lower in my own eyes than at any time before, and showed me the emptiness of all my gifts, left me neither power nor will, so as I became as a weaned child I could now no more look at what I had been or what I had done nor bee discontented for lack of strength or assurance. My eyes were only upon his free mercy in Jesus Christ. I knew I was worthy of nothing for I knew I could do nothing for him or for my self. I could only mourn, and weep to think of free mercy to such a vile wretch as I was. Though I had no power to apply it to myself yet I felt comfort in it.

I did not long continue in this uncertain condition, but the good spirit of the Lord breathed upon my soul, and said I should live. Then every promise I thought upon held forth Christ unto me saying I am thy salvation [*Psalm 35:3*]. Now my soul could close with Christ, and rest there with sweet content, so ravished with his Love, as I desired nothing nor feared anything, but was filled with joy unspeakable and glorious [*I Peter 1:8*]. Not that I could pray with more fervency or more enlargement of heart than sometimes before, but I could now cry my father with more confidence [*Romans 8:15*]. Me thought this Condition and that frame of heart which I had after, was in respect of my former condition like the reign of Solomon; free, peaceable, prosperous, and glorious, the other more like that of Ahaz [*another of Israel's kings*], full of troubles, fears, and abasements.

The more I grew thus acquainted with the spirit of God, the more were my corruptions mortified, and the new man quickened: The world, the flesh, and Satan, were for a time silent, I heard not of them: but they would not leave me so. This estate lasted some months, but not always alike, but if my comfort, and joy slackened awhile, yet my peace continued, and it would return with advantage. I was now grown familiar with the Lord Jesus Christ. He would often tell me he loved me. He lay down with me, and usually I did awake with him. Now I could go into any company and not lose him: and so sweet was his love to me, as I desired nothing but him in heaven or earth.

This condition declined slowly. As worldly employments and the Love of Temporal things stole away my heart from him, so would his sweet Countenance be withdrawn from me. But in such a condition he would not long leave me, but would still recall me by some word or affliction or in prayer or meditation, and I should then be as a man awakened out of a dream or as if I had been another man. And then my care was not so much to get pardon, for that was sometimes sealed to me while I was purposing to go seek it, and yet sometimes I could not obtain it without seeking and waiting also, but to mourn for my ingratitude towards my God, and his free and rich mercy. The Consideration whereof would break my heart more, and wring more tears from my eyes, then ever the fear of Damnation or any affliction had done; so as many times and to this very day a thought of Christ Jesus, and free grace bestowed on me melts my heart that I cannot refrain from weeping. Since this time I have gone under continual conflicts between the flesh and the spirit, and sometimes with Satan himself. But still when I have been put to it by any sudden danger or fearful Temptation, the good spirit of the Lord hath not failed to bear witness to me, giving me Comfort, and Courage in the very pinch, when of my self I have been very fearful, and dismayed. My usual falls have been through dead heartedness, and presumptuousness, by which Satan hath taken advantage to wind me into other sins. When the flesh prevails the spirit withdraws, and is sometimes so grieved as he seems not to acknowledge his own work. Yet in my worst times he would yet support me that my faith hath not failed utterly.

The Doctrine of free justification lately taught here [*by John Cotton and amplified by Hutchinson*] took me in as drowsy a condition, as I had been in (to my remembrance) these twenty years, and brought me as low, I thought, as if the whole work of finding assurance of salvation had been to begin anew. But when the voice of peace came I knew it to be the same that I had been acquainted with before, though it did not speak so loud nor in that measure of joy that I had felt sometimes. Only I found that I had defiled the white garments of the Lord Jesus [*Rev. 3:4,5*]: that of Justification in undervaluing the riches of the Lord Jesus Christ and his free grace, and setting up Idols in my own heart, some of them made of his Silver, and of his gold; and that other garment of sanctification by many foul spots which Gods people might take notice of, and yet the inward spots on my garments of sanctification were fouler than those.

The Lord Jesus who (of his own free grace) hath washed my soul in the blood of the everlasting Covenant, wash away all those spotts also in his good time. Amen, even so doe Lord Jesus.

JOHN WINTHROP

SAMPLE CONVERSION NARRATIVES

In the mid-1630s, the Massachusetts churches began the practice of having prospective church members describe to the entire congregation their process of conversion. In most instances, the prospective member addressed the church members directly, and the church members were free to pose questions. Occasionally, female church members would give their statement in private to the church elders.

The following narratives were given by prospective members of Thomas Shepard's church at Cambridge. Shepard took them down himself, while making no effort to create an exact record of the speaker's words. His notes are extremely terse, and it is sometimes impossible to decipher the speakers' meanings from them. Shepard was among the fiercest opponents of John Cotton and Anne Hutchinson. He emphasized that doubting and struggling with sin were excellent signs that one had been saved, and he was probably most likely to have recorded those parts of the narratives that fit in his framework of salvation. Applicants for admission to his church also probably knew that it was not a good idea to talk too much about raptures around him. In the Boston church, Anne Hutchinson's allies might have voted against applicants who gave narratives with so many doubts. What follows are fairly free adaptations

The narratives are from Thomas Shepard, *The Confessions of Diverse Propounded to Be Received & Were Entertained As Members*, New England Historic Genealogical Society, and are used with permission. They have been published in George Selement and Bruce C. Woolley, eds., *Thomas Shepard's Confessions, Colonial Society of Massachusetts Collections* 58 (1981), from where we have taken the biographical information, and Michael McGiffert, ed.,*God's Plot: The Paradoxes of Puritan Piety* (1994). More conversion narratives are available from those sources.

Nicholas Wyeth

[Nicholas Wyeth (born 1595?, died 1680) emigrated from Suffolk, England, to Cambridge, Massachusetts, in 1638, with his wife and child (another died during the voyage). He was a mason and farmer. This confession was from 1645. Wyeth's is a dramatic account of a loose teenager slowly being drawn to a puritan life. His chief sin—it seems—was that he "profaned the Sabbath much." In other words, he spent Sundays having fun with his friends rather than worshipping God. But this changed when he was about 16. Awakened to his sinfulness by powerful puritan preachers, he would travel many miles to hear their sermons. This was characteristic of puritans. Also characteristic was how it got him in trouble. English law required that you stay in your own parish on Sundays and listen to your parish minister, regardless of whether or not you felt you benefited from him. Under Archbishop Laud, the law was increasingly enforced. When Wyeth was arrested, he decided to go to New England, "where we might enjoy more freedom." Friends, who probably did not like puritans, tried to convince him that God was angry at him for this decision. Notice how—many years later—Wyeth remains filled with doubts about himself as he gives his story. He repeatedly emphasizes that he sees one sign of sanctification in him in his desire to be with good Christians. At the same time, he admits that he has a hard time paying attention in church and does not feel himself full of zeal. He is clearly not sure if he has been saved. Note too that some questioners are

skeptical while others are more encouraging.

The church decided to admit Wyeth. Perhaps they decided that his continual self doubts were a sign of true Christian humility, and perhaps too Wyeth deep down thought the same. His great desire to join them was itself a sign that he was among the saved.]

NICHOLAS WYETH'S NARRATIVE

It pleased the Lord to show me the evil of not keeping the Sabbath. Around 16 years old and an apprentice, I was keeping idle company. The Lord helped show me the way out of that, 16 of Ezekiel—'None eye pitied thee [but] I said unto thee when thou wast in thy blood, Live.' I understood that the Lord was the refuge for pity. But I had profaned the Sabbath much, and although the Lord showed me that I was wrong and had profaned, I was still troubled with what I had done.

But there were no powerful preachers where I lived, and I wanted to hear what was most suitable to my heart. Going to hear Mr Salby, I was very moved by his ministry. The word was so powerful that I realized that I was lost and that the words of God could help me. And the Lord encouraged me to go and hear other ministers. So every Sabbath for a year I went four miles to hear him. I took every opportunity I could to get permission from my master to go hear. Though I did not improve much, I had great love for hearing sermons and loved the society of God's people.

I lived that way for twelve years until the Lord brought Mr. Burrows to preach some 16 miles away. I was in good health and I went often to hear him. I heard him say out of Galatians: 'as a man sows, so shall he reap.' He showed that a natural man who has not been converted did not sow anything that was good, everything was evil. And I saw that I was in my natural condition yet went to see another preacher 20 miles away, and although I heard much, my heart was not brought as near to God as I would have wished because I was careless in remembering what I heard. And I went on like that for 16 years in England. Then I was persecuted and brought to court for hearing sermons outside my parish.

Hence I came to New England where we might enjoy more freedom. I had much joy in going about this work of emigrating. Though I had lived very foul, my heart strongly convinced me of the error of my ways and that I should live where there was a powerful ministry. My friends opposed me and the enemies of God discouraged me. God took away my son, and some people told me that this showed that God was displeased with my plans to emigrate. But I paid no attention to the discouragement of natural [unconverted] friends. My wife too was going through many troubles, but I did not care even if the Lord took away all I had. I believed that if the Lord should bring only me and my child here, He would recompense me. When we arrived, the Lord raised up my wife, and I did much rejoice to see the place and see the people and hear God's servants.

Though I have been much tempted with the idea of moving to another colony, yet I saw so much of the love of God's people here that I thought I would bring much evil on me if I left. But the Lord's hand has been much against me and is still. He gave me a child after my own heart and has taken it from me. It is just, for I have gone on formally and coldly since I came here. Though I have had the great spiritual advantage of the public church services, I have been very unfruitful and unchristianlike.

Interviewer 1. Do you remember nothing of how God has offered Christ to you?

N. Wyeth. In Ephesians 2, I heard that ye who sometimes were far off are made near by the blood of Christ. The lord showed me that the only salvation is his free grace.

Interviewer 1. What effects did it work?

N. Wyeth. His free grace encouraged me to go on and showed me that I had nothing in myself.

Interviewer 1. Did the Lord ever give you assurance of his love in Christ?

N. Wyeth. The Lord let me see that if I were not born again, I could not enter in the Kingdom of God.

Interviewer 1. What supports the hope of your heart?

N. Wyeth. Nothing but free grace in Christ. I feared that I should not be able to speak the truth but it appears that I have been unprofitable. I wanted to be in the society of God's people.

Interviewer 2. What ground of assurance do you have?

N. Wyeth. Because love began [to the brethren]. [Puritan ministers offered this as one of the most reliable signs of sanctification. See, for example, 1 John 3.14.].

Interviewer 2. How do you know that?

N. Wyeth. Because I see good in them and would get good from them and therefore think myself unfit to come into their society.

Interviewer 2. Have you no fears?

N. Wyeth. Yes, death in regard of unprofitableness, unsensibleness of my condition and want of assurance.

Interviewer 3. You complain of unsensibleness. You say that is caused by drowsiness? Is there no other evil but that?

N. Wyeth. I have a wandering eye, not attending upon the word preached in sermons. I have not made use of God's people to get into their societies.

Interviewer 3. Are you not one unfruitful tree that should be hewn down?

Interviewer 3. You rejoiced much when the Sabbath came?

N. Wyeth. Yes but I was sleepy at the same time. On the Sabbath I would have a great hope to see what I have not yet seen about Christ and that hope caused me to rejoice, yet it has been with a great deal of deadness. I labor against it and have striven against it and have hoped that the Lord would meet with me.

Interviewer 4. What did you mean when you said you comfort yourself with vain hopes?

N. Wyeth. Well though I went to hear the minister with much expectation, I have heard as unprofitably as before.

Interviewer. What have you read or heard that might make you hope the Lord might meet with you?

N. Wyeth. I believed that listening to sermons and prayer was the means to the Lord, and so I knew I was in the right way because "draw near to me and I'll to you" [loosely James 4:8].

Interviewer. Would the Lord deny you?

N. Wyeth. There is nothing lacking in him but only in myself, yet I have comforted myself in waiting upon the Lord.

Interviewer. What benefit have you had from God's ways?

N. Wyeth. I have seen more of the love of the Lord Jesus by such truths I have not heard in old England, as how to observe sabbath and prepare for it and others which I cannot speak. I have much of Christ's love and being supported and hearing of his love has brought me in awe of his will.

Interviewer. Have you seen into your heart and life any more?

N. Wyeth. Yes, out of commandments.

Interviewer 4. Then there is something of fruitfulness [in you].

Interviewer. What use make you of Christ regarding sin?

N. Wyeth. I knew out of John: 'without me you can do nothing.'

Interviewer. What is your foremost secret desire?

N. Wyeth. That the Lord would manifest himself more to my soul in Christ and in the power of ordinances.

Interviewer. Why do you forget things, brother?

N. Wyeth. I see cause enough in my own heart why the Lord should deny me. I know many things in my practice. I have not so meditated on the word.

Francis Moore

Francis Moore (1586-1671) came to Cambridge with his wife and two children at some time in the 1630s. Moore worked as a tanner and held a number of minor town offices. Although he was poorer than average, he was much esteemed in Cambridge for his piety. Eventually, he became an elder of the church, the highest position a layperson could hold.

Moore's narrative is a fascinating example of the long, roller-coaster process of trying to find assurance through self-scrutiny. Moore first tried to figure out whether his repentance for his sins was proof of genuine sanctification. For a while, he convinced himself that it was. Soon he fell into doubt again, so he examined himself with another question: Did his sins leave him with a general detestation of all sin? He thought that they did, so again he concluded that he must be saved.

But temptation proved too strong for Moore. He began to grow complacent, and as he did, his vigilance against sin relaxed. He stopped observing Sunday strictly, and from there it was a short step to loose company and drinking. Yet every time Moore succumbed to temptation, he came back again to the ways of the Lord, with renewed determination. That determination convinced Moore that he was among the saved, and it satisfied the congregation. In an odd way, Moore concluded that God must truly have loved him—and God's love was surely tantamount to God's grace—because God kept reaching out to pull him back from sinning. This formulation, too, bothered Anne Hutchinson.

However, it must be remembered that the congregation knew Moore and so had independent ways of satisfying itself about the genuineness of Moore's struggles.

FRANCIS MOORE'S NARRATIVE

The Lord revealed my miserable estate to me, but I found the flesh resisting the Lord and contradicting Him. Then the Lord showed me that without repentance none could be saved and that there must be sorrow for and hatred of sin. I started to repent for my sins. Now when the Lord had gone this far with me, I questioned whether my repentance was right or no, or whether it went no farther than the repentance of Cain and Judas [*both Cain and Judas showed horror for their sins, but were damned*].

But seeing that I did not only leave evil but cleave to the contrary good, I concluded that there was a genuine work of God in me. Many doubts soon arose. But the Lord showed me that Christ came to save those that were lost (Matt. 18:11), not only in general sinners, but myself. And hereby the Lord wrought farther humiliation and sorrow for sin past. And then applying that promise, those that mourn and hunger shall be comforted and satisfied (Matt. 5:4, 6), here arose that question whether I did truly mourn under my misery or not. Now here the spirit of God sealed to my soul [*showed me*] that I was truly humbled, not only broken for, but from, sin with detestation of it. Hence, I was a new creature and hence was saved and received to mercy.

Since that time the Lord hath made my estate more clear. Yet I still committed many sins. Being assured of salvation, I grew careless and neglected the Sabbath. Then the Lord forsook me and I fell into loose company and so to drunkenness. And then the Lord broke my soul the more for what I had done.

My sinning made me question whether ever this saving work was wrought in my soul or not. How could I depart from God after such infinite love? Yet the Lord set on that word, though he had such a heart to abase his grace, yet that the Lord was unchangeable in himself and so in his love, and that Christ has come to seek and save those who are lost.

Yet after my relapse in sin I conceived it was not possible the Lord should pity me. Then I heard—to him that believes all things are possible (Mark 9:23)—and that, though I had backslid, yet returning to the Lord, here was rich love. This drew my heart to the Lord again because his love was unchangeable.
Other relapses I still find in myself as security and sloth and sleepiness and contenting myself to go to church services without feeling the good of them. Yet the Lord calls me back again. I mourn after every relapse, and I know that my mourning is genuine because it endears my heart all the more to the Lord and makes me conduct myself more humbly.

Brother Crackbone's Wife

The given and maiden names of Brother Crackbone's wife have not survived. The Crackbones came from London and were moderately prosperous. Gilbert Crackbone joined the Cambridge church about four years before his wife did. Goodwife Crackbone's extraordinary account of how she reached assurance is a dramatic example of the puritans' ability to see God's purposeful activity in the world around them and tie it to their own inner lives.

BROTHER CRACKBONE'S WIFE'S NARRATIVE

My brother sent for me to London in a good house. There I considered my course and ways, especially of one sin. I thought the Lord would never accept me, and I was terrified and out of hope. But hearing 1 Isaiah—though your sins be as scarlet, they shall be as white as snow—I had some hope. But I was married and poor and my child was sick. The Lord took my child from me. I was troubled and feared that the child might go to hell because I had not prayed for it.

And so I came to New England. But I forgot the Lord as the Israelites did after He had led them to the Promised Land. When I had a new house yet I thought I had no new heart. And attending church did not do me any good, and so I doubted of all the Lord had done for me. I thought of seeking after the sacraments, but I did not know whether I was fit for church membership [only church members could take the sacraments]. Yet I heard in a sermon that without being a church member, I was only under one of the wings of Christ, and not yet under both. [*She can listen to preaching (one wing) but since she is not a church member, she cannot have the benefits of the sacraments or church discipline (the other wing).*] I saw in myself sloth and sluggishness, so I prayed to the Lord to make me fit for church fellowship and for the Lord Himself. But the more I prayed, the more temptation I had, so I gave up. I was afraid to sing a song of thanks to the Lord [*this could be a reference to any number of psalms*] because it might be that I was singing a lie. Then I recalled the verse Lord, teach me, and I'll follow thee [*roughly Psalm 86:11*) and I heard that the Lord will break a sinner's will as His last work before conversion. When I saw my house burned down, I thought it was just of God to take it from me, and merciful of Him to spare the lives of my children when I had again not looked after them properly. And as my spirit against him was fiery, it was fitting that He burned all I had. Hence I prayed that the Lord would send the fire of His word and baptize me with fire [*Matt. 3:11*]. And since then, the Lord has set my heart at liberty.

Appendix C: Recommended Reading

GENERAL INTEREST

Darret Rutman, *Winthrop's Boston: 1630-1649* (1964).

Michael P. Winship, *The Times and Trials of Anne Hutchinson* (Lawrence, KS, forthcoming, spring 2005).

SPECIALIZED TOPICS

Economic Issues

Barnard Bailyn, *The New England Merchants in the Seventeenth Century* (1964).

Darren Staloff, *Making of an American Thinking Class: Intellectuals and Intelligentsia in Puritan Massachusetts* (1998), chapters 3 and 4.

Louise Breen, *Transgressing the Bounds: Subversive Enterprises Among the Puritan Elite in Massachusetts, 1630-1692* (2001), pages 50-55.

Gender Issues

Michael Winship, *Making Heretics: Militant Protestantism and Free Grace in Massachusetts, 1636-1641* (Princeton, 2002).

Selma R. Williams, *Divine Rebel: The Life of Anne Marbury Hutchinson* (1981).

Lyle Koehler, "The Case of the American Jezebels: Anne Hutchinson and Female Agitation during the Years of the Antinomian Turmoil, 1636-1640," *William and Mary Quarterly* 31 (1974), pp. 55-78.

Elaine Huber, *Women and the Authority of Inspiration: A reexamination of Ttwo Prophetic Movements From a Contemporary Feminist Perspective* (1985).

Amy S. Lang, *Prophetic Woman: Anne Hutchinson and the Problem of Dissent in the Literature of New England* (1987).

Mary Beth Norton, *Founding Mothers and Fathers: Gendered Power and the Forming of American Society* (1996).

Other

Alfred A. Cave, *The Pequot War* (1996).